THE NEXT BEND IN THE RIVER

Gold Mining in Maine

C. J. Stevens

JOHN WADE, Publisher
Phillips, Maine

Copyright © 1997 C. J. Stevens

Published by
JOHN WADE, Publisher
P.O. Box 303
Phillips, Maine 04966

First Edition Published 1989
Second Edition Published 1997

All rights reserved. No part of this book may be reproduced, stored in a retrieval system, or transmitted in any form or by any means, including electronic, mechanical, photographic or magnetic, without prior permission in writing from the author or publisher, except by a reviewer who may quote passages in a review.

Library of Congress Cataloging in Publication Data
The Next Bend in the River
#97-62354

ISBN 0-9623934-1-X

Second Edition
Printed in the United States of America

Acknowledgments

I wish to thank Ed Quirion of the Weld Inn in Weld, Maine for suggesting that I write this book, and to Gary Howard of Bath for supplying encouragement and information.

Without the assistance of the following people this book never would have been realized. I owe them all a special word of thanks for granting me interviews and providing materials: Helen Barker, Alton Bradford, Charles Bragg, Carrie Bristol, Edwin A. Churchill, Charles Damery, Rodney Davis, Forrest Dexter, Glendon Dill, Richard Doyle, Edward Ellis, Adam Galuza, William Garrett, Bob Goodrich, Lester Gould, Ed Hamilton, D. Priscilla Higgins, Arnold Howe, Irene Hutchinson, Esther Knapp, Kenneth Knapp, Lee Knapp, Stuart Martin, George Mattor, Ann McCrillis, Dean McCrillis, Richard Minear, Tom Miner, Roland L. Moore, Gerald Morrison, Harvey Packard, Jerry Perrier, Rosey Perrier, Ellis Quinn, H. Bud Quinn, Phyllis Quinn, Stanley Voter, Virginia Western, Greg Willet, and Ona Willet.

I thank the following for photographic illustrations: Dan's Photo Service, H2 Photographers, Lil Giant Photo, William Mattor, Willis Davis and Greg Willet.

I am grateful to Mason Philip Smith, The Provincial Press, and Greeley's Mill Cartography for the cover layout.

Acknowledgements are made to these libraries: Dixfield Public Library, Farmington Public Library, Maine State Library, Mexico Public Library, Rangeley Public Library, Rumford Public Library, and the University of Maine Library (Farmington).

I owe a special debt of gratitude to Maine Geological Survey, Maine State Museum, Oxford County Mineral and Gem Association, Rangeley Historical Society, and the Rumford Area Historical Society.

To the publishers or copyright holders of the following books: *The Adventures of Buckskin Sam* by Buckskin Sam; *The Minerals of New England* and *The Mines of Maine* by Frank L. Bartlett.

Further acknowledgments are made to these publications: *Aroostook Pioneer, Bangor Daily News, Boston American, Boston Herald, Boston Post, Dixfield Citizen, Down East Magazine, Franklin Journal, Houlton Times, Kennebec Journal, Lewiston Evening Journal, Lewiston Sun, Maine Life, Maine Minerals, Maine Mining Journal, Maine Mining and Industrial Journal, Maine Postal History, Maine Times, Oxford Democrat, Portland Evening Express, Portland Press Herald, Rock & Gem, Rockland Courier-Gazette, Rumford Falls Evening Herald, Rumford Falls Times, Rumford Citizen,* and *Yankee.*

BOOKS BY THE AUTHOR

Poetry
Beginnings and Other Poems
Circling at the Chain's Length
Hang-Ups
Selected Poems

Biography
Lawrence at Tregerthen (D. H. Lawrence in Cornwall)
The Cornish Nightmare (D. H. Lawrence)

History and Adventure
The Next Bend in the River (Gold Mining in Maine)
Maine Mining Adventures
The Buried Treasures of Maine

Animal Behavior
One Day With a Goat Herd

Fiction
The Folks from Greeley's Mill

CONTENTS

THE NEXT BEND IN THE RIVER

Gold In Maine

"Would you like to see a nugget from the state of Maine?" This is what I ask people when they stop to look at my wife's gold and tourmaline jewelry display at shopping malls, craft fairs, and festivals. Then I open my hand and show them the piece of gold I found on the East Branch of the Swift River in Byron, Maine. The nugget weighs a little more than half an ounce—about twelve pennyweights, half the size of my thumb—and I consider myself lucky to have found it. One visitor at our *Maine Gold* booth offered me a thousand dollars for it. "It's not for sale," I replied, and as I closed my hand and stepped back from the table, aware that I wasn't even tempted by the offer, I realized that selling the nugget would have been like trying to forget the thrill I had when seeing it for the first time in my gold pan.

If someone had suggested to me ten years ago that Stella and I would be selling jewelry and giving demonstrations on how to pan and sluice for gold, I would have called that person crazy. But we didn't know a decade ago that we both would get gold fever and the direction of our lives would change.

Even as a small child I was aware that there were precious metals and minerals in this part of New England. I had heard stories about people risking their lives in old mine shafts, and I wish now that I had listened more closely. But a great-uncle who was fond of telling these tales had the reputation of stretching the truth from Kittery to Fort Kent.

I suppose most people know that Maine is unusually rich in minerals. Those who stop at our display don't appear surprised when we tell them that some of the finest tourmaline in the world comes from Oxford County. But gold is another matter. So many are unaware that the state has a history of such mining activities.

"I didn't know there was gold in Maine!" This is a frequent remark, and it amuses me when I see those looks of astonishment as I assure them that flakes of the metal can be found in many Maine rivers and streams.

"I tell you there isn't any here," said an irate middle-aged man at the Lobster Festival in Rockland, "and nothing you can say is going to convince me otherwise!" I still can't figure out why he got so upset when I showed him the nugget. "Don't you think I know better than that!" he growled while looking at me accusingly. "I was born and raised here." I further complicated matters when I tried to soothe him by saying that the University of Maine at Augusta had offered gold panning courses on the Swift River for several summers and that there was a fine collection of Maine nuggets at the state museum. This information only made his face more purple. "It isn't true!" he shouted as he turned away in disgust.

We seldom get reactions this vehement. There are those people who have no interest in gold, even if a productive mine were found in their backyard. "It would ruin my lawn," declared an elderly gentleman at the Bangor Mall. Probably the comment that amused me most came from a tall, well-dressed woman at the Clam Festival in Yarmouth. She looked at the nugget, and with no expression on her face and in a flat, tired voice said "Whoopie."

Response on the whole to the idea of gold and a mother lode somewhere in Maine is decidedly positive. We often have a crowd four rows deep around our table, men, women, and children, all wanting to hear more about our prospecting adventures. It is something they would like to do themselves. At times, we get so caught up in relating our experiences on streams and rivers that we forget we are there to sell Maine gold and tourmaline jewelry.

Then someone in the crowd will begin telling a long and involved story about an abandoned mine a relative once stumbled upon in the deep woods, or how a grandfather in his early manhood found a vein of gold in quartz. Such discoveries are usually made when the parties are out hunting and it is fast getting dark. Of course the sites can never be located again, and the treasures are still out there somewhere.

I am sure these veins thicken and the shafts grow longer over the years in the telling. But there is always an element of truth mixed with the exaggerations. People do find excavations in the woods all over the state, and one has only to study mining records of the past century to realize how promising gold once was as a major Maine resource. If all the local gold hunters were counted, from the time of the returning forty-niners to the present recreational dredgers, the numbers would forever dash the misconception that there is little to look for here in Maine.

Geologists have known for years that there are two ancient volcanic belts in this state which contain lead, zinc, copper, silver, and gold. The major belt stretches from the Maine-New Hampshire border into the Maritime Provinces, and the minor belt runs from Penobscot Bay to the New Brunswick coast. Reports that no sufficiently high-grade ore has been found to make mining an economic feasibility in these belts are false. Amounts assaying higher than some productive mines in the Western states have repeatedly been found in Maine. As recently as the late 1970s, substantial copper deposits were found at Chase Mountain near Patten, and Bald Mountain, west of Ashland. There was talk of a billion-dollar mining industry in Maine and some geologists were hoping to see gold and silver deposits exposed as these two mines developed. But cheaper imported metals drove down the price of the domestic supply in the early 1980s. The Blackhawk Mine in Blue Hill closed in 1978 as did the Harborside Mine near Castine the previous year.

Low-flying planes with magnetometers have explored thousands of acres in Maine. By measuring the earth's magnetic intensity in the folds and faults of the planet's crust, valuable mineral deposits can be detected. The wilderness areas of the state have been crisscrossed with such doodlebug devices, but these operations are not always successful. It must be remembered that only two percent of Maine's bedrock has ever been exposed. Not all the facts are in yet. The presence of gold and other metals is usually found in the topsoil. Soil tests are taken, and if there is enough of a certain metal traced a test boring is done. But locating gold is expensive, regardless how one prospects, and finding it is a matter of luck.

There are about seventy-five old gold mines in Maine. They are scattered throughout the state and have been abandoned for years. Yet gold mining is still going on along the coast of Newfoundland and in the St. John's area of New Brunswick. The types of rocks found in these two locations are similar to formations in Maine. Since there is gold there, the question must be asked: Why not here? Well, it can be found in Maine. Traces of gold are present in almost any deposit of pyrite and other sulphides. In Blue Hill, Hamden, and Dexter, for examples, places where such minerals have been mined, gold has appeared in fairly encouraging quantities.

One prospector, who stood talking by our display table at a fair, and who called geologists working for the State of Maine "bureaucrats," also pointed a finger at local newspapers and regional magazines. He felt that the publishing trend has been to give gold hunting a bad press—particularly placer mining which is described as a sort of harmless hobby that can't be taken too seriously. I had to agree with him when he lambasted journalists for headlining their gold articles with the tiresome expression "There's Gold in Them Thar Hills!" More than a quarter of the two hundred articles I collected in libraries and archives around the state while researching this book carried such a banner. The trend has been, when featuring a prospecting story, to present the material with some condescending slant, such as, Mr. Jones pans gold because his wife needs a new wedding ring, or Mr. Smith wants to improve his health.

Most geologists claim that Maine doesn't have a dense belt of gold, and that anyone who mines in this state and expects to get rich is dodging reality. But Greg Willet of Rangeley, who has operated several successful claims in the West, thinks that "Maine is on the verge of having a gold boom." Willet is convinced that he will "be mining profitably within the next three years."

Until recently, the only gold information available from Maine's Geology Department in Augusta was a single sheet listing the streams and rivers where traces of gold could be found. The possibility of lodes has mostly been ignored. Aside from human interest articles about panners and dredgers, little attention has been given to the placer mining scene.

It would be pointless to mention all the locations where gold can be found. Most Maine residents can find microscopic traces of it on their own properties. But some towns do have greater concentrations. An example would be the Appleton-Rock Pond area which has long been known as a gold producer. It has given fair wages for short periods of time to a number of prospectors, and there is a source promising enough for future placer mining.

Other locations frequently mentioned include Acton, Albion, Andover, Anson, Augusta, Baileyville, Baring Twp., Barney, Bethel, Blue Hill, Brooksville, Calais, Caratunk, Carmel, China, Columbia, Concord, Corinna, Cutler, Dallas Plt., Dennistown, Dover Foxcroft, Ellsworth, Emden, Etna, Franklin, Gardiner, Gouldsboro, Greenville, Guilford, Hamden, Hancock, Harmony, Harrington, Haynes Twp., Hiram, Houghton, Jackman, Jackson, Lebanon, Lemoine, Lincolnville, Livermore, Lowell, Lubec, Madrid, Marshfield, Milton Plt., Minot, Moose River, Moscow, Mount Vernon, Newfield, New Portland, New Sharon, Orland, Orrington, Palmyra, Paris, Pembroke, Penobscot, Pittston, Phillips, Prospect, Rangeley, Readfield, Rockport, Rumford, Saco, Sandy River Plt., Shirley, Skowhegan, Sorrento, Southwest Harbor, Strong, Steuben, Sullivan, Surrey, Swan's Island, Vinalhaven, Waterboro, Willimatic, Winterport, Winthrop, Woodstock, TWP 3R5, TWP 5R2, and TWP 5R6.

But the area that has received the most attention during Maine's 135 years of placer mining, and the place where every serious gold hunter in the state eventually visits and often remains, is Byron. The East, West, Main, and Stockbridge Branches of the Swift River provide a never-ending supply of coarse and fine gold. Without a doubt, the East Branch has the richest yield. It has long been recognized as the most productive stream in Maine, and it is here that many of the early gold mining adventures took place.

Location of placer gold areas in Maine. Each indicated by a circle.

Byron

There are reports that gold was first discovered in the United States on the Swift River, but most records show that Maine's first gold was found in 1854 on Perham Stream in East Madrid. One often hears the story of a small nugget appearing in the crop of a chicken that a Byron resident was dressing for Sunday dinner. No one can be sure just where or when traces of color were first seen. The early settlers were writing about Indians who wore nuggets around their necks. What is known about this part of Northern New England is that gold has been washing down from the hills since the time of the glaciers.

Swift River Pond in Franklin County is where the Main Branch rises. The pond is at an elevation of 2,216 feet. This mountain stream tumbles down 1,755 feet through Byron, Roxbury, and Frye before emptying into the Androscoggin River at Rumford. The Swift is only 25 miles long, but 120 square miles of land is drained. Somewhere in this area a lot of gold is hidden. The river is well named. It cascades over rocks and through canyons, and during the spring floods one can hear the thunder of boulders rolling along the bottom beneath the floating ice and debris. Surrounded by sizable hills, Byron has unusual scenery. Tumbledown Mountain is one of the most spectacular views around. There are several peaks rising in height of more than 2,700 feet, and just east of Weld is Mount Blue.

Called Skillerton by the Indians, Byron became a town in 1833. It was named for Lord George Gordon Byron, the English poet, whose death had occurred a few years previously. The hillsides are covered with spruce, and years ago this led to the profitable business of making spruce gum. In fact, a part of Byron, at Coos Canyon, is still called Gum Corner.

Among the first prospectors to pan gold on the Swift River were five men who left their homes in Upton, Maine during the 1849 gold rush in California. Having little luck, they returned and decided to mine the East Branch in Byron. Their reason for selecting this stream was that the rock formations closely resembled those found in California. The names of these miners were Wood, Norcross, Cleaves, Whitney and Robinson. Whitney's first name was Marshall, and his son, Perley, became one of the best known prospectors in the history of Maine's placer mining. Little is known about the other four men, but it is said that Norcoss became ill and was taken in by a Mrs. Reed, who tried to nurse him back to health. Records show he died in Roxbury and was buried in the Byron Cemetery. The man had no relatives, and not unlike so many of his fellow forty-niners, Norcross was penniless at the time of his death.

Several years before the turn of the century, Byron was being invaded by an army of gold hunters. Fred Fowler of Rangeley remembered riding on the Rumford Falls and Rangeley Lakes Railroad when he was a small boy. The train was too heavily loaded with goods to make the steep grade before going into Bemis. The engineer had to back down to Houghton to get up steam.

"Along the Swift River at Houghton and Byron," wrote Fowler years later, "gold had been discovered and the stream was lined with a number of tents. People were along the river bank panning and while the train waited for steam, the prospectors were plied with questions. One old fellow said, 'Gold? Why the River's full of it! I panned nigh unto ten dollars wuth t'other day.' " Such a report made an impression on young Fowler and he vowed he would "pan a couple of thousand pounds himself some day."

Perley Whitney

It was in the late fall of 1889, shortly before the snow, that Marshall Whitney and Perley left Upton on a trip in search of better trapping grounds. When the two got to Coos Canyon, they were convinced that here was a gold-bearing stream equal to any they had seen in the West.

Marshall had a sizable collection of nuggets he had saved from his gold days in California, and of his two sons, Perley was the one who took an interest in mining. Jesse was more like his mother, Insom Leibby Whitney: these two preferred life on the farm. Mrs. Whitney felt that gold hunting was a "frivolous and risky calling," and someone had to stay home and care for the livestock. When Marshall went West again to work around the gold mines, he took Perley with him. The young man, who was born in 1865 and was 20 at the time, worked as a cook's helper. When he wasn't busy preparing grub for the crew, he learned to grind samples in the assay office and gained knowledge on how to recover gold in free milling ore. Perley always claimed that he got his start in life because the chief assayer at the mine was lazy and liked his booze.

After studying the river at Coos Canyon, Marshall and Perley drove their buggy through Byron Notch into Weld and stopped for the night at the first farmhouse. When supper was over, they had a long talk with the farmer. He told them about a person who camped in the vicinity every year. This man hired the farmer to take his gear into Byron Notch, but the visitor didn't want to reveal just where he was going with his provisions. After a couple of weeks, the man would return to the farm.

Marshall and his son asked their host what he thought the man was doing. The farmer didn't know, but he guessed it had something to do with some yellow stuff, some yellow rocks. Were they heavy? "Oh yes!" said the farmer. "Terrible heavy!"

Perley glanced at his father, and the subject was quickly changed. They weren't surprised, but they both knew that they had to get on the river as soon as possible. The place where they would try first would be the East Branch. This they talked about, over and over, as the heavy snows drifted around their Upton farmhouse. Tired of waiting for the first signs of spring, Perley and Marshall pitched a tent on the frozen river in March and began prospecting.

During their first week, after shoveling snow, breaking ice, and axing clay from a ledge, they found about 25 cents in color. Marshall Whitney smiled at his son and said: "Now we know there is gold here." That summer, according to several estimates, the Whitneys collected more than a $1,000 in nuggets. Perley admitted to Maine gem and gold prospector C. F. Marble that on one spot by the East Branch—and Marble was convinced that the report was true—Perley and his father found about $3,000 in gold in two years, all of it within a stone's throw.

It was only a few months after they began mining on the Swift that Marshall Whitney saw a farm he liked on Buckfield Hill overlooking the East Branch. His wife and Jesse were still in Upton, but the pull that the river was having on Mr. Whitney was enough to convince him that the Upton property must be sold. In C. E. Marble's article of 1951, in the *Oxford County Mineral and Gem Association's 40th Anniversary Yearbook,* the story is told.

"Perley was left to keep watch, while his father went back to raise the money." But another person was also interested in the farm and had sent a young man to make a better offer. Then the young fellow started back to Bethel in his jigger, a two-wheeled buggy, to get the necessary cash.

"When the elder Mr. Whitney got back with the money, the old fellow refused to sell—said he had bargained too cheap. Mr. Whitney was very angry, and started off with Perley hanging on his arm—'Father, Father, wait a minute, let me talk to him.' " The disgruntled Whitney relented, and the son went back to reason with the man. The owner was going to raise the price a hundred dollars.

"Perley's father went down to Roxbury," wrote Marble, "and borrowed the extra money from Mr. Reed (and later paid it back in a gold coin made from Byron gold, as told to me by Mr. Reed.)"

But again the farmer refused to sell. It was a Friday and no business transactions could be made on that day. It was bad luck.

"So the next day they were there before the old fellow had eaten his breakfast, took him down to Roxbury to a Notary Public, and completed the deal. When they came out the door putting the papers away, the fellow in the jigger came along, horse on the run and dripping lather, yelling, 'Hey, hey, wait a minute before you sell!' But it was too late."

After the Whitneys settled on the farm, Perley was away from Byron for several years. But he did visit his parents frequently enough to court Clara Taylor who lived nearby on Buckfield Hill. They were married in 1896 in Rumford Falls, Maine. Perley was 30 and Clara 17. Though they lived together for several years before separating, the marriage was never a happy one. Perley moved his young bride to the Lewiston area and opened a jewelry shop across the street from the old Littleton Hotel. There he repaired clocks, fashioned rings and designed covers for watches.

It wasn't a good time in his life. Perley loved the outdoors too much to get any real satisfaction from his jewelry business. He felt confined, and the memory of his months on the river left him restless. He wasn't gold crazy; he didn't dream of finding huge nuggets—both he and his father looked upon prospecting as a business. But as time slipped by and his marriage deteriorated, he became depressed and people stopped coming to his shop. Then his brother left the farm and his father died. His mother was now alone. When he and Clara decided to end their marriage, Perley went back to Byron to look after his mother and to hunt for gold.

Perley Whitney, 1901

There have been many stories told about this man and the treasures he found on the Swift. Over half a century has passed since his death, but Whitney exploits increase with the telling. It doesn't take much to twist the truth if the tale comes from someone suffering from gold fever or from a journalist looking for material to decorate a Sunday newspaper feature. Perley's name has appeared so often in print that it is now nearly impossible to separate what did and didn't happen. One exaggeration can be traced to a remark Whitney once made: "I estimate that $20,000 worth of gold has been taken from the Swift River." It wasn't long before the claim was being made that Perley had taken that much from the river within a period of only a few years.

Perley Whitney was the sort of man who wouldn't stifle a rumor if it was in his favor. Gold he found, and plenty of it—probably more than any other person, with the possible exception of Carl Shilling, though they weren't of the same generation. Whitney did have the advantage of being on the Swift when there was more gold to be found. But one never knew about a Whitney nugget. Was it something his father had found in California, or a piece he cleverly created from some old watch or chain? When asked who was the better miner, Shilling or Whitney, those who were acquainted with mining on the Swift thought it was Perley. Carl Shilling worked harder, they all agreed, but in knowledge of gold and locations Whitney was given the edge. "He never dug the hard way for it," said Adam Galuza of Woolwich. "He looked for the good spots. Those that other people overlooked."

"He was a very intelligent man," remembered Galuza. "Perley told me a lot about the places where he found gold." Then Galuza spoke of a location on the East Branch. "It was halfway up where the German (Shilling) had his camp. There was a little series of waterfalls. Perley took a hand sled up there one fall on the snow and he came back with a basketful of dirt and he panned it out in his house and at $32 an ounce it was worth $500."

Whitney once admitted to Maine newsman Sam Connor that if his year's findings were averaged, he made only a decent day's pay. On this occasion he claimed the most he ever got from one pocket was $400. Perley told Connor that mining engineers from California, South Africa, and Australia had looked over the Swift River. These experts agreed there were good indications of gold, but the results wouldn't justify investing huge amounts of money.

Perley got to know the river better than anyone because he was methodical and kept records. He could tell one not only how much gold he found on any given day but the exact spot and its particular yield. In time, he was able to come up with a theory of his own, and he put it in these words: "It is necessary to learn the bedrock of the area so that when one pocket with gold is found, the formation will direct the miner how to go ahead with a reasonable assurance of locating another."

"Perley had some gold that he showed me," recalled Helen Barker of Turner, Maine. "But after seeing the gold that my father got from the East Branch, it looked different." Then Mrs. Barker paused before going on. "I did hear the story, when I was a young kid—and it was laughed at a lot—that he melted gold and shot things in the river and people flocked there. Now this is a story. I don't know if it was true or not."

One of the more popular tales of Whitney's mining activities describes how he would go out at night with his lantern and come back the next day with enough gold to buy his groceries. Sometimes he was followed on the East Branch, but he had a way of disappearing behind a boulder. He was once seen with a magnifying glass, and he was picking gold from a crevice in a rock.

Helen Barker remembers going over in the evening with her sister, Irene, and visiting Perley. This was in the thirties when he was living in Houghton, on the road to Rangeley. Mrs. Barker's father, Frank Ferrin, was Perley's nephew.

"I must have been thirteen and my sister was seven years younger. We enjoyed listening to him." Mrs. Barker recalls the house being very cluttered. "He had a lot of watches, and he had some kind of magnifying glass set on his table. He would be going through his gold, and he would tell us stories, like how he would go and get deer. He said he had a white sheet that he fixed around himself, and he could walk in the wood very quietly and carefully.

He was able to go right up where the herds were."

Whitney distrusted people, and he often wanted to be left alone. "A cantankerous old fellow is the only way I would describe him," said Kenneth Knapp, a former Byron resident. But Perley also had a need to be with others, and he loved to talk. Sometimes he would get out his fiddle and play a few country tunes and sing. Then his lighthearted mood would pass. He was not one to trifle with, and any people having dealings with him had better say exactly what they meant.

Once, when he left his house unattended, someone broke in and took some of his things. He was outraged, and he told the Ferrins that it would never happen again. Any person breaking into his place should be prepared to pay the penalty. The next time, before he left his house to be away overnight, he propped a loaded shotgun in a chair and attached a string to the trigger and to the door. "That bastard can stop by all he wants now," said Whitney.

"Uncle Perley was a person who would talk with you," recalled Helen Barker, "but he was very careful what he would tell you. He was cautious and suspicious of people."

"I remember going over there," said Kenneth Knapp, "and he'd greet me and everything, but one didn't want to touch anything. 'Don't prowl around,' he'd usually tell you. 'Don't touch that! Don't touch that!' Then he'd tell you to keep away from his shed. He said he had a bear trap out there."

Perley Whitney was a tall, thin man, and he had only one eye. Each of his shotguns had an addition on the stock for the other shoulder—he preferred using the same trigger finger after his eye injury. But people around Byron claimed that he could see more with his one eye than others could with two. Show Perley a piece of gold, his neighbors were fond of saying, and that bad eye would open in a hurry.

Walter Galuza and his brothers were logging next to Whitney's land, and Galuza got permission to use the edge of Perley's field for loading the logs. It was agreed that the place would be cleaned up by a certain time, but the date came and went and nothing was done. Perley saw Galuza about the matter. "Yup, yup, I'll clean it up," promised Walter. "I'll give you just thirty days, Mister," said Whitney. A month went by and the logs remained. Perley strapped on his old pistol and visited the logger. "Walter Galuza, the thirty days are up. You've now got just twenty-four hours!" Galuza tried to stall: "There is a law," he began...."This is my law," snapped Whitney, tapping the gun. "I want that wood out of there now!" It was Galuza who told Kenneth Knapp the story. "You know that old fellow meant business," said Galuza. "I got the crew together, and we got the wood the hell out of there!"

Whitney bought an old touring car in the twenties, and the way he drove it irritated everybody. He never exceeded twenty miles an hour, and it was impossible to get past him because he kept to the middle of the road. Finally, he got into an accident and totaled the vehicle. There was a sigh of relief all over town, but the time for celebrating was premature. Immediately, Perley got himself new wheels, and this car he drove about fifteen miles an hour. Within the year there was another collision. It was then that Whitney decided that the roads around Byron were too dangerous for him.

"He used to go out into the woods and pick herbs and certain grasses," said Adam Galuza. "My mother had awful headaches—so bad she had to walk with a chair. We told Perley about it, and he said: 'I'll fix that.' So he made her a tea and she drank half a cup and never had a headache again for the rest of her life."

Helen Barker remembered that she never saw Perley sick, and he never had colds. But the man did pay dearly for working so many years in icy waters without waders. Near the end of his life, he had to hire others to get his gold for him. His ankles were numb and his circulation poor.

But it didn't stop him from fishing along the Swift River. "I went there once to Whitney's camp," recalled Dean McCrillis of Roxbury, "and he had been arrested for having short fish. Five hundred of them. They decided they had better get him on that one."

Perley had a piece of quartz that was close to three inches in diameter with wires of gold streaked through it. He tied the quartz to a section of thin rope that was hooked to the wall in the kitchen by the stairs. Adam Galuza claimed that on one of his visits he saw this and also a jar filled with gold nuggets. The pieces of gold had a silver content and looked whiter to Galuza than color found on the Swift River. Whitney said the quartz with wires of gold came from within twenty minutes of his house. Galuza remembers sitting in the living room and listening while Perley pulled the nails from a step going upstairs. This was where the jar of nuggets was kept.

"I never saw that piece of quartz," said Kenneth Knapp, "but I've heard of it—you hear all sorts of things. Some said Perley used to take jewels out of a watch and put in a substitute. I've also heard about a quart jar of nuggets, but I would doubt that a man could lift a jar of nuggets that size."

"You don't have to worry about me," Whitney told the Ferrins when they began to see that his health was declining. If he ever needed help, he would hang a red bandanna outside his door. "I can look after myself."

Kenneth Knapp didn't see any signs of Perley, and there was no smoke coming from the chimney as he drove his school bus past the house. On one of his trips, Knapp went up to the door and knocked. There was no answer, and the curtains were drawn.

"I got after my father-in-law, Frank Ferrin," recalled Knapp. "I said: 'Come on, Frank, let's go see.' 'To hell with you!' he said. 'You don't know that old fellow the way I do! If you did, you'd keep the hell away from there!' " But Knapp felt something was wrong. "So I went to see Roy Dow who had the hardwood mill," recalled Knapp. " 'Damn right,' he said. So we went down, and before I could do anything, Roy hauls off and breaks the glass and reaches in and unlocks the door. We found the old fellow in bed, stiffer than a board. They figured he'd been dead at least a week."

Kenneth Knapp warned the medical examiner and the others to watch themselves when moving the body. "You may find a German Luger," said Knapp, "and it will be ready to use." Sure enough, under the pillow, as it had been throughout his life, the loaded gun. Whitney's place of burial was in the Frye Cemetery, outside Rumford, and the date was January 20, 1941.

After his death, gold hunters descended, and the house was torn apart. Carrie Bristol, who bought the place in 1965, stated that the interior walls and ceilings were demolished. There wasn't a board or brick left untouched. Even the shed was ransacked.

"Probably the piece of quartz was taken," said Adam Galuza, "but about the jar of gold, I don't know. Maybe he'd dug a hole in his well and buried it there. Perley once told me the well had a sandy bottom. After he died, when the windows were broken and the doors were left open, I went in there and lifted the step with a screwdriver. I took a flashlight and looked down there, but there was nothing."

Kenneth Knapp, like Galuza, had heard that the gold might be in the well. But Carrie Bristol was surprised when hearing this rumor. "There isn't any well, and there never was one. We have a spring down back with a tile."

After moving into the Whitney house, Mrs. Bristol went over the grounds with a metal detector. She found old car parts, empty cartridges, and even the front end of an old train with a cow catcher. The best finds were pieces of copper with names on them. Whitney had been practicing engraving. One copper plate had the name of the Oxford Mining Company, the date it was chartered and the year it was dissolved.

"I went into the bank when I first came here," said Carrie Bristol, "and I wanted to start a checking account. When I told them where I lived, the first question was: 'Have you found any of the gold?' It was my time to laugh because I had already been approached so many times about it."

The Oxford Mining Company

The Oxford Mining Company is still remembered around Byron. Some residents appear amused when the firm is mentioned and others are embarrassed. Perley Whitney knew the company's reputation when he engraved its name on scraps of copper plate. Perhaps he was thinking that such souvenirs would have commercial value.

It all began one day in 1905 when Timothy Boudreau, a mining engineer and printer from Manchester, New Hampshire, called on John Houghton in Byron. The reason for the visit was land. Boudreau was interested in 240 acres along the Main Branch of the Swift River. After the usual amount of talk and dickering, Houghton agreed to sell the land for $1,200. The two men hurried to Rumford in a buggy, and papers were signed.

Then Boudreau took the train to Lewiston to see his old friend and fellow miner, J. A. Delisle. They had prospected along the Main Branch together, and both knew the river well. Would Delisle be willing to become a partner? Boudreau outlined what he felt should be done with the property. He really needed someone with mining experience. Pleased that Boudreau should come to him, Delisle immediately agreed to take part in the venture.

The two men organized the company, and stock was made available to the public. Certificates were printed in Boudreau's shop in New Hampshire. Soon the peaceful little settlement of Houghton on the road to Rangeley was scrambling with activity. Not since that day when the train backed into town to get up steam, and Fred Fowler saw the tents along the Swift, had there been such excitement. Two heavy crushers went into action, and a dozen men were hired to run the machinery.

Boudreau and Delisle were quick to promote their new company. They were smooth talkers and both had talents for finding investors. Certificates were being sold at astonishing speed. Samples showed traces of gold, and this multiplied by more than two miles of riverbed encouraged many people to open their pocketbooks. Then Boudreau and Delisle began to speak of a mother lode hidden in the cliff by the river. Boudreau told the stockholders at a meeting that there might well be more than glacial gold from the Pleistocene epoch awaiting them. The investors were impressed with Timothy Boudreau's knowledge, and they were sure that here was a man who was going to make them all rich.

Delisle and Boudreau called on Perley Whitney to get his views on mining. They knew he was an expert in such matters, and Perley didn't deny it. Finally, the two got down to the real purpose of their visit. Would he lend them some of his nuggets? They wanted to show people what Swift River gold looked like. It was a strange request, and one that made Perley feel uncomfortable. He was interested in their gold operation, but he didn't want to part with his choice pieces. Papers would be signed, Boudreau assured him. Finally, he gave in and lent them some. It was only later that he learned that the two had used his gold to help sell stock. Perley was outraged. He strapped on his pistol and confronted the miners at their site. If they didn't return his gold at once, he would expose them as frauds to the stockholders. Delisle told him that they had intended to return the nuggets that very day. "I'll save you the trouble of coming over," said Perley Whitney.

The mill was completed, the riffles installed for processing, but the results were disappointing. The gold caught in the porous schist was all on the surface. There was nothing to worry about, Boudreau told his nervous investors, steps had been taken. A tunnel was being drilled into a mass of quartz under the cliff.

Then one night when hanging clouds made Houghton its darkest, when no one was around the crushers, shotgun charges of gold were blasted into the rock. "Gentlemen," said Boudreau with his usual glibness, "we are on the verge of a real discovery!"

The Houghton Post Office thought so too. Listed in the book *Maine Postal History* was a new town: "Goldfields, Oxford County, Byron, 1909 and 1910." Boudreau and Delisle had put a new town on the map. But it would be only for a short time. When their mining adventure was exposed as a hoax, Goldfields, Maine quickly became Houghton again.

By the time the certificate holders began asking questions, and several rumors of fraud were adrift in Byron, Boudreau and Delisle had sold $150,000 in stock. Late in 1910, federal officers descended on Goldfields and officially closed the plant. The two mine operators were arrested on the spot, handcuffed, and transported to Concord, New Hampshire to await trial. The charge was using the mails to defraud.

At the March term of the New Hampshire U.S. Supreme Court, in 1911, both Boudreau and Delisle pleaded not guilty, but during the trial they changed their pleas to nolo contendere, throwing themselves on the mercy of the court. Delisle was fined $1,000 and Boudreau $2,000. Timothy Boudreau was also given a six month jail sentence.

The Oxford Mining Co. Site

Perley Whitney was asked to appear in Concord as a witness. He testified before the court, and the morning after the trial, while waiting at the station, he saw the Delisles. They, too, had come to catch a train but not the one back to Maine. "They didn't look at all prosperous," wrote C. E. Marble, after hearing the story from Whitney, "in fact a bit sloppy, and then the old lady got up and put on an act. She walked around wringing her hands and moaning and taking on, 'Me, I don' lak dis contree. She don' be ver' good contree. Me I'm go back to Canadaw. She's good contree that one.' Perley said he knew right then that she had the money in a roll under her garter. He said he found out later that they bought a fine large farm outside of Montreal and settled there."

Today, one can still see the indentation in the cliff. At first glance, and considering all the years of erosion, one wonders if this was made by man. The terrain up the river to the site is rough and there are waterfalls. Gold panners occasionally brave the boulders. There are no big nuggets washing down from the hills, no mother lode here. But maybe, if one looked long enough in this shallow cave at the river's edge, one could still find a few shotgun flakes of color in the quartz.

Buckskin Sam and Napoleon Bonaparte Jackson

The Swift River has had its share of colorful personalities. Timothy Boudreau was a warm and open person, but he swept people along like broken twigs in a spring flood. Boudreau swindled a lot of investors who believed in him. In his case, the crime is remembered but not the man.

Buckskin Sam and Napoleon Bonaparte Jackson are looked upon differently. Both were characters, and on a few occasions only a step or two ahead of the law, but they are remembered with smiles and even with a sort of fondness. Though the two have been dead for years, they are sometimes mentioned in Byron as if they were still in the vicinity and hunting gold on the river.

"A kind of Buffalo Bill" was how George Mattor of Otisfield, Maine described Buckskin Sam. Sam did resemble William Cody when dressed in his buckskin coat and vest and cowboy hat. He was a proud man and totally self-centered. Buckskin lived in a camp in nearby Bemis, and when he worked, which wasn't all that often, he hung wallpaper and trapped.

Sam wrote a book about his early days, and since he did have a high opinion of himself, he called it *The Adventures of Buckskin Sam*. "Nearly killed by a man-eating tiger, pursued by Indians, all these reported by him before he was twenty-one." This was how Stuart Martin of Rumford Point, Maine described the book and Sam's many exploits. "He was a real phony," said Martin with a grin.

Buckskin was that and more; he made himself a legend. He knew how to stage a dramatic scene. In his book, Sam tells the tale of his last great bear fight in the town of Byron in 1898. *The Adventures of Buckskin Sam* was privately printed and became a local sensation.

He frequently was seen panning gold along the East and Main Branches, and it is surprising that he didn't make claims of finding the mother lode. No one knew if he ever found much color, but there are a few people around Rumford who still recall what some of the old-timers said about Buckskin's talents as a miner. "He got all his gold when he came to town—he didn't pan it; he just lied about it."

Then there was the California and Black Hills prospector with the impressive name of Napoleon Bonaparte Jackson. He lived for a number of years on a point of land with the Swift River on both sides. "Bone" or "Bony," as he was called, built his own cabin and constructed a bridge that could be raised and lowered.

Jackson made a living of sorts by teaching gold panning in the summer and collecting spruce gum in the winter. Those who remembered him claimed that he was so addicted to chewing the gum that he often lost a tooth. This was saved and hung with the others on a string above his table in the cabin.

He was a familiar sight along the banks of the river. When he came across some greenhorn gold panner or a fisherman, he would reach deep into the pocket of his trousers and pull out a handful of nuggets. This was Swift River gold, he would tell them. Nuggets found not too far from where they were standing.

Perley Whitney told Adam Galuza that Jackson was an "old so and so," and the gold Bony kept pulling from his pants was from California. It didn't have that warm, rich, Swift River color. But there were a lot of panners who took Jackson seriously, and they rushed to the spots where he said gold could be found. "They'll be lucky if they find a speck," said Perley.

"Bony was quite a character," said Kenneth Knapp. "I've heard my father tell how tourists would go see him and ask if he could take them out and show them how to find some gold. 'Oh yes,' he would say. 'I guarantee it!' " Jackson chewed tobacco, and when no one was looking, he would stuff a bit of gold in his mouth along with his chaw. "He'd start panning," said Knapp, "and would spit in his pan, and the gold would be right there!"

Adam Galuza got his first gold mining lesson from Jackson. It was no secret that Bony liked his booze, and one year the Galuza cellar had an ample supply of hard cider. "Don't you give him any," warned Mr. Galuza before leaving for town. "His wife throws a fit when he gets tight!"

Adam's father was no more than out of sight before the boy opened the front door and found a thirsty Napoleon Bonaparte Jackson. Adam was fourteen at the time and long had been interested in mining. Would he like to learn the art of gold panning? asked Jackson. A splendid deal could be made. Two jugs from a big barrel seemed like a bargain to the young man.

"When we got to the river," remembered Galuza, "he waded across to where a rock jutted out. He had a crowbar and he took some rocks apart and he came back and sat on the bank and started panning. When he got to the black sand, there was a nugget about as big as a pea and another one a little smaller. So I went to reach for the big one and he says: 'Oh, that's no good,' and he throws it back into the water. 'Let's go home,' he tells me. 'I've showed you how to pan for gold.' "

Likable as he was as a person, Jackson wasn't always an easy man. His temper frequently flared. "In listening to all these stories about him," said Stuart Martin, "I get the impression that it wasn't difficult to pick a fight with Bony."

Rumors still persist that Napoleon Bonaparte Jackson died under mysterious circumstances. He had gone West for a few years and came back with enough money to purchase a farm outside Rumford where he planted a large orchard of apples. Adam Galuza heard that Bony was murdered, and his charred body was found in a pit where brush had been burned. Some people said Jackson raided a sluice box on the Swift, and he was killed in revenge.

Stuart Martin remembered reading an article stating that Jackson "had been done away with over a dispute on a piece of land on a site on Mount Zircon." But Martin, distrusting this version, asked Jackson's granddaughter if the story was true. "And she said no. He planned his death himself. So you've got that controversy."

The coroner's report ruled a suicide, but it isn't surprising that Napoleon Bonaparte Jackson should depart from this world leaving rumors behind him. Wherever he went, whatever he did, his presence was felt, and he delighted many with his antics. One can easily imagine that what young Adam Galuza didn't see on that outing were two small nuggets being pocketed by an eccentric and flamboyant man who was thinking hard about cider.

Will Arris, Indian Joe, and Dominic

Will Arris lived in Byron and prospected on the Swift River for many years. He suffered from palsy later in life, and it was said that he found his ailment helpful when he went gold panning. All he had to do was hold the pan in the water and his shaking would do the rest.

Will was a good friend of the Clarence Youngs in Byron village, and Young's granddaughter, Irene Hutchinson of Dixfield, Maine, remembered the visits. "He used to come over, and there was always a checker game going on. We children used to love to watch him light his pipe—it took the longest time to get it going."

Arris was remembered for his bright-red handlebar mustache, and he was an old railroad man who worked for years on the freight runs going in and out of Oxford County. After his retirement, he had difficulty remembering things. Will Arris would drive to Lewiston in his automobile, park the vehicle on the street, do the shopping, and come home on the train.

He knew the better spots on all the branches of the Swift, and his collection of nuggets was impressive. Two were more than a quarter of an ounce, and how he stashed his findings made them even more memorable. He carried his gold around in the thumb of his kid glove.

"He was an old character," recalled Irene Hutchinson with fondness in her voice. Then she spoke of Arris coming back from the river with a big catch. "I know he used to go down and take every fish in Mary Knapp's little pond and it would make her so mad!" But soon his friends learned why he was so lucky. "He shook so when he held the pole," said Mrs. Hutchinson, "and the fish would just take the bait."

Another miner on the river was Indian Joe. He was in and out of Byron for a number of years and came from the Berlin, New Hampshire area. One summer he made himself a birch-bark hut by an old railroad bed on the East Branch. It was in the same spot where Carl Schilling would later build his camp. But most of the time Indian Joe stayed behind Clarence Young's house in the village. Indian Joe was well aware that his birch-bark shelter was on the site of an old placer mine. Perhaps one of the reasons why he and Carl Shilling never got along was that they both knew there was gold along the bank.

Ellis Quinn of Byron remembered hearing about the placer site. It was the time when the Blanchard and Twitchell Railroad was building the line along the East Branch. "One of the men had been out in California and recognized the spot as a possibility for gold," explained Quinn. "They quit the railroad and made a year's pay in a short time."

Indian Joe was handy with a gold pan and he could cook and make things. Irene Hutchinson told how he was often whittling spoons for her mother's kitchen. One of his specialties was a stick to take doughnuts out of the fat. "He would show up every now and then," said Mrs. Hutchinson. "I remember he didn't have any hair on his head, and he looked real Indian. Dark. A very pleasant guy."

Dean McCrillis recalled fishing with his grandfather, Clarence Young, and visiting Indian Joe on the East Branch. Mr. McCrillis hadn't forgotten that day when he caught a twelve inch trout. His grandfather saw Indian Joe standing on the old railroad bed near the hut. "We went up," said McCrillis, "and he asked us in to eat with him. I think he had squash and potatoes. It wasn't much, but it filled us up, and we gave him our fish. I hated giving up that trout!"

Byron is a place where miners come and go. Not every prospector on the river gets to know those who live in the village. But Indian Joe was one who became friendly with several families, and his gentle ways soon made him a favorite. Then one summer he drifted away and never came back. Now, after all those years, people around town still are wondering what happened to him.

Even more mysterious was the disappearance of a gold hunter known as Dominic.

It was the year of the big hurricane, 1938, and early in the season for mining. Frank Ferrin looked out of his window just as a Rumford taxi came into the dooryard. A short, stocky man with black hair got out of the cab and came to the door. He introduced himself and explained that he had come to the Swift River to look for gold. The man told Ferrin that he needed a place to pitch his tent. He didn't want to camp back in the woods because of a heart problem. Could he rent a space behind Ferrin's house? He had his own supplies and promised to be careful with fires.

Frank Ferrin, who was a kind and generous man, liked the looks of the stranger. It was a nuisance having someone so near the house, but he felt certain that here was a person who wouldn't be a problem. Just to be safe, he did warn his daughters, Helen and Irene, not to get too friendly. "I know nothing about this man," he warned the girls. "You say hello and be polite, but don't you two go running out there."

Ferrin is now dead, and no one in the family remembers Dominic's last name. The squatter kept to himself most of the time, but he was friendly. He soon established himself on the river, up on the East Branch by a clay bank. He would walk up early in the morning, look for gold all day, and come back to his tent before dark to cook dinner. He seemed to be an active man for someone with heart trouble, thought Carl Swantee, a miner who enjoyed visiting the Ferrins in the evening after a day of prospecting. "We didn't get to know him," remembered Helen Barker, "but he was a nice man. If he went down to get groceries in Roxbury, he usually came back with a bag of candy for us."

Then one day Swantee met Dominic on the river. It was just before the hurricane, and the sky was threatening. "It's going to blow, and blow like hell," Carl warned him. "You better get ready and cut your tent ropes. It's a big storm, you wait and see."

Dominic did go back to lower his tent, but instead of asking if he could stay with the Ferrins, he packed a knapsack, took a piece of canvas with him, and went to the ledge by the clay bank on the East Branch. Swantee saw him climbing the steep slope.

Dominic didn't return to his tent after the storm, and when several days went by with no sign of him, Ferrin began to worry. "You don't suppose he got buried under all that clay?" he asked Swantee. "I wish you'd check it out for me." But Carl Swantee found no trace of a landslide.

Then a few days later, when their parents were in Rumford shopping and the Ferrin girls were home alone, Dominic reappeared. "I want to go back on the river, but I don't want to be by myself." It wasn't one of his better days, he told them. "Will you girls go with me?" Irene looked at her sister as Helen shook her head. Remembering their father's warning, the two made an excuse. Dominic went back to his tent and soon disappeared.

The man was gone again, and Ferrin was troubled because nothing had been taken from the tent. "You don't suppose he got lost up there?" he asked Swantee one evening, "or a bear got him or his heart played out?" Then, a few evening later, Carl Swantee had an unusual story to tell the Ferrins.

"I ran into Dominic today," said Carl. "He was hungry, and I gave him some of my sandwiches." Swantee had noticed that the man was terribly excited about something and was having trouble keeping it to himself. "OK, Dominic, what is it?"

"I found it! I found it!" He had followed a brook high above the East Branch to where the water plunged over a ledge. There was a bar of gold going across the stream under the fall. "I found it, and I'm going back!"

Swantee and the Ferrins never saw Dominic again. "He wasn't seen by anyone," recalled Helen Barker. "All his equipment was left out behind the house." Finally, before the snow came, Frank Ferrin took down the tent and stored the gear in his shed. There it stayed, never to be claimed. "No one knows if the gold was ever taken from the stream," said Mrs. Barker, "and that's all I know about Dominic."

Byron in the Nineteen Thirties

Many of the miners who came to Byron in the thirties weren't there for weekend outings. Better wages could be made with a gold pan than by working on some road gang or in a hot hayfield. A dollar a day was the average salary for laborers during the Depression. Even with gold at $32 a troy ounce, some panners could find the equivalent of a week's pay in one crevice, and a fair-sized nugget could put groceries on the table for two or three weeks.

"You find a lot of young fellows up here," Clarence Young told a reporter in the late thirties. "They bring a tent and cooking utensils and pan all day. One of them told me confidentially that some days they would get four or five dollars' worth, and then they would go a day or two without getting any. But they do well for themselves." Young was often asked by newcomers to take them prospecting. It was a request he seldom turned down. He loved the outdoors, and his knowledge of the river was considerable. "I even remember him panning gold in the winter," said his granddaughter, Irene Hutchinson. "He used to bag his black sand, and he would sit by the fire and pan gold in a washtub."

Clarence Young

Another miner who did well on the Byron scene was Lionel Bartlett of Buckfield, Maine. He used to pay his taxes with Swift River gold. Like many prospectors of that time, Bartlett trapped in the winter and went gold hunting as soon as the water was bearable in the spring. Charlie Bragg of Buckfield remembers riding to Byron in Bartlett's Model A. "I thought we'd never get up there," said Bragg. "Every time he saw a bottle on the side of the road, he had to stop and pick it up. He was the kind of man who would take a penny out and turn it four ways before spending it. That fellow got some good gold."

Some impressive nuggets have been taken from the Swift. Carl Swantee was one of the lucky miners. He prospected in Byron for fifty years and found more than his share. Swantee was an outgoing person, and he and Clarence Young were close friends. Carl loved to fish, and though he never got as many trout as Will Arris, Swantee knew the better pools on the river. Before his death, he donated his gold to the Maine State Museum; in the collection was one piece weighing 18.5 grams, nearly a thumb-sized nugget.

In the late thirties, there appeared a Massachusetts man on the Stockbridge Branch. Like Dominic, he stayed only one summer and disappeared. The man hired Peter Paul, an Indian who lived in Roxbury, to dig for gold. Peter Paul was paid $10 a day, an unheard of salary for shovel work at that time. The visitor cleaned the riffles of the sluice by himself and put the concentrates in old whiskey bottles without looking for signs of color. When the season was over, the bottles were crated and shipped out of Rumford. Peter Paul was told that he would be needed again the following year. But that was the end of it.

"Clarence Bateman knew all the old-timers," said Charlie Damery of Old Orchard Beach, Maine. "He's been coming to his property here in Byron for nearly fifty years." Bateman, who lived in Columbus, Ohio, built two small cabins along the East Branch and turned some of his acreage into a tree farm. He spent many summers working as a director at Camp Kawanhee, a boys' camp in nearby Weld. One of the highlights of the season for him was when he took the boys panning on the Swift. Bateman held mining classes for thousands of youngsters, and many of them returned years later with their families to hunt gold again.

The scene began to change noticeably in Byron by the early forties. The Depression was over, and the country was at war. One saw fewer miners. Perley Whitney was gone, and though Swantee, Young, Arris, and Joe White, who rented gold pans at Coos Canyon, were all active, there were no outsiders camping along the river. The one who did the most prospecting now was Carl Shilling. He had built himself a place halfway down the East Branch by the old railroad bed and was keeping to himself.

Carl Shilling

Carl Shilling was born in Germany on September 9, 1888, the son of a vegetable and poultry farmer. Carl and his two brothers, Paul and August, helped market the family produce while political tensions increased around them. When Paul was inducted into the army and got a severe foot infection from so much marching, Carl decided that the military was no place for him. At seventeen, he and a boyhood friend fled Germany and signed a contract to work for a year in the mines of South Africa. Carl's job was operating a drill under appalling conditions. The two young men soon regretted what they had done, but there was no way they could break the contract. When the year was over, they left without looking back.

What happened next in Carl's life isn't known, and he never wanted to talk about it. He always changed the subject or fell silent when asked about this time in his life. He let slip a few details over the years to people he knew well in Byron, but Carl was definitely hiding something. Not until he was an old man did he allow his photograph to be taken. He would turn his back when someone came near with a camera. Shilling told the Youngs that he had come to this country legally, but all his identification papers had been stolen shortly after his arrival. He did speak of working as a tree surgeon in Syracuse, New York, and later as a gardener for a hospital near Boston. From these two jobs he was able to save enough money for trousseaux for his sisters, Helen and Mary, in Germany. He went to night school to learn English, drifted away from Boston, found work with a bobbin company in Lewiston, Maine, and came to Byron sometime in the early thirties.

There has been much speculation about what really went on in Carl's life between the time he left South Africa and his appearance in Syracuse. It has been said that he was a deserter from the German army, a cook on a German submarine, and an escapee from a prisoner of war camp in Maine. There is even the possibility that Carl went to Brazil—many Germans were going there during and after World War I.

Why did this man live the life of a recluse down the East Branch of the Swift? Why suddenly, after forty years of turning away from the world and having contact with only a few neighbors, does he buy himself an 8 mm camera, poses happily in photographs, and wants people around him? Perhaps a threat had been removed or an old enemy had died.

Carl worked in the woods and found jobs around Byron for a few years before dismantling a building on Buckfield Hill and carrying the lumber down the East Branch to build his camp. He was strong and willing to work, but every job he did had to be done his way. People didn't tell Carl what to do. If they did, he would get angry and leave. He saved enough money to manage for long periods of time, and he panned and sluiced for gold throughout the summer months. When he had to work again, Carl found more odd jobs and helped Clarence Bateman build two camps. Bateman also hired him to go on field trips and to teach the Kawanhee youngsters how to pan gold.

World War II wasn't the best of times for Carl. Some people in Rumford and Mexico, Maine, suspected him of being a spy. After all, the country was at war, and there were those who sympathized with Hitler. Radio reports of a huge Nazi gathering in Madison Square Garden in New York City just before the war didn't help Germans like Carl who lived in remote areas.

Clarence Young, who was one of Carl's friends but who sometimes fell out of favor, went down and told Carl that he would have to surrender his radio. Mr. Young was sorry, but there had been talk. Carl was outraged. He had done nothing wrong. "If you want my radio, you can have it!" he told Young. It was then that Carl put it on a chopping block and smashed it into a hundred pieces. "Here is your damned radio!" he said.

Vegetables and flowers crowded Carl's garden, and everything he planted grew in profusion. He seemed to know the right balance of nutrients for the soil and how much water the plants needed. But what amazed those who stood admiring his garden was how symmetrical everything looked. Nothing was out of line. His rows of flowers, string beans, carrots, and squash were all in place. Signs of East and West, North and South, were placed as general compass directions about the garden. Even the ginger ale and brandy bottles decorating a table outside his camp made a colorful column.

Carl's experience as a gardener in Boston served him well. A waterwheel, powered by a hose set in the brook above his camp, was a convenience when there was little rain. The wheel tumble polished the stones while a line from the hose watered the plants. He enjoyed sharing his vegetables with friends, and even during that time in his life when he wouldn't let anyone take a picture of him, Gordon Brown of Buffalo, New York, had no difficulty photographing Carl proudly holding a huge squash.

"I remember those apple brandy jugs," said George Mattor while watching one of Carl's 8 mm films. "Ellis Quinn had a liquor store on Cape Cod, and he used to give them to Carl, filled with apple brandy. The jugs were left outside on the table all winter because he didn't have any place for storage."

Another neighbor, Rodney Davis, claimed that some of the best wild apples around came from Shilling's root cellar. Carl occasionally slept out there on hot summer nights. Sometimes, in December or January when the temperature plunged dangerously, two kerosene lanterns were kept burning in the cellar.

"He had a big buck deer in there one time," said Mattor. "This was before the season. 'Come here! Come here!' said Carl. 'He's a good one eh! He's a nice one!' It was an eight-point buck, only partly hung up because the cellar wasn't high enough."

For many years, before the cost of groceries began to increase noticeably, Carl could live on fifty cents a day. He would stock his cellar with staples for the long winter months, and because he had a hearty appetite, he would buy twenty- and thirty-pound joints of meat. Some of this he would put into glass containers, using the same rubber jar rings over and over. Visitors who watched him opening these jars wondered why he hadn't already died of ptomaine poisoning.

"I had deer meat out of one of Carl's jars," said Rodney Davis, "and it scared me half to death. 'It won't hurt ya,' he told me. 'But Carl,' I said, 'you killed that deer in November and this is April.' The meat was a little salty but it tasted all right. I don't know how he did it."

Arnold Howe of Falmouth, Maine, who came to Byron often and prospected with his friend Joe Porthier, remembers how meticulous Carl kept the place. "We'd go down there and eat lunch with him and have some of the bread he baked—the best I've ever had. We would sit on the floor because the ceiling was so low. Carl was a very short man, barely five feet."

Many of Carl's friends enjoyed going to his camp in the winter to watch him feed the various flocks that came to his seven feeders. He had a special way with blue jays. "Aah, aah!" he would cry, and they would come from all directions. George Mattor recalls as many as thirty in the yard where Carl had scattered bread crumbs. Then, when it was time to give the others a chance, Carl would rap on his window and the blue jays would leave.

Carl Shilling Buttering the Limbs Courtesy of Stanley Voter

He always made sure that his chickadees had a special treat. On winter days, he smeared margarine on the bushes around the yard. He greased the limbs generously, explaining to Stanley Voter, who photographed him rubbing a branch, that a thick layer of margarine stayed longer than suet and didn't blow away.

"One year we carried three hundred pounds of bird food up there during the winter," said Carrie Bristol. "He'd strew birdseed all the way to town, and the birds would be there to meet him where he left off on the way back. It was so funny."

Carl had fixed a bell near the feeders. The bell had a small rope attached to it, and the rope went into his cabin through a hole he had drilled. Whenever Carl saw a squirrel raiding one of the feeders, he would pull the line and ring the bell. It amused him to see the squirrels running away in fright.

But he hated the hawks that swooped down off the mountain to chase his birds. It angered him whenever it happened. One day after a hawk had made several swings through his yard, he went outside and waited with his shotgun. When the hawk circled back, Carl fired. The shot missed the bird but not his cabin. "Hee, hee," he would say to people visiting him and pointing at the hole, "I scared that hawk!"

Carl would spend several hundred dollars when shopping in Rumford in the late fall. He would sometimes store his groceries with the Youngs in Byron and leave camp once a month to get his social security check cashed and to take back kerosene for his lamps. He had become good friends with Clarence Young's son and daughter-in-law, Norman and Lenna. In her article about Carl, in *Maine Life,* Lenna Young remembered that he would give her his trading stamps. Only cash was real to Carl, not pension checks and store coupons.

He always tried to get his winter supplies into camp before it snowed. But one year the snow came early. George Mattor and his fifteen-year-old son carried more than 500 pounds of provisions from the bottom of Dingle Hill in the village all the way to Carl's. It was a full day's work. "There would be fifty or sixty pounds of sugar and sixty or seventy pounds of flour," recalled Mattor. "He was grateful for the help, I guess, but he never offered to pay."

Mattor, and others who cared for Carl, didn't expect to be compensated. When asked if they didn't at times feel that he was taking advantage of their kindness, not one of them said yes. They all knew his ways. If he asked them to go to town and to bring him a five-pound chicken, he expected just that, not a four-pound or a six-pound bird. If there was *Tide* on his grocery list, one didn't come back up the trail with *Rinso.*

Carl Shilling's Camp Courtesy of William Mattor

Mattor recalled another animal incident. A bear, sniffing about the cabin, caught the smell of something in Carl's root cellar—it then crawled on the roof and fell through. This was probably the same bear Carl had seen by his tumbler one day. The bear was leaning over the waterwheel, and the sound of the stones in the tumbler fascinated the animal so it was turning its head with the motion of the wheel. Mattor was amused and asked what Carl would do if he met the bear when walking up the trail. He didn't hesitate for a moment before replying. "I'd say, you get the hell out of there! That's my path!"

If a piece of jasper or quartz caught his eye, Carl would polish it in the tumbler. He kept an assortment of stones on his porch, and when panners came back to his camp they would buy from him. It was Carl's way of getting paid. Mining lessons were free, unless some financial arrangement had been made in advance. Herkimer diamonds, beryl, agates from Nova Scotia, stones that Carl's friends didn't know what to do with, were placed on sale.

Helen Barker, who often visited Carl, thought he made beautiful things and was more talented in jewelry making than Perley Whitney. But not everyone cared this much for Carl's creations. Stanley Voter remembered meeting two men coming up Bateman's Lane. They had been down to see Carl and one of them had purchased a Herkimer diamond pendant for three dollars. "Hell, that's no good!" said the man, pulling it from his pocket and throwing it into the woods.

As he got older and the winters seemed longer to Carl, he looked forward to visits from Diane and Carrie Bristol, the Lee Knapps, and others in Byron. When he heard the sound of snowmobiles on the trail, Carl would usually come out of his camp and wave them down. But if he didn't like the looks of a person, even if the stranger was with someone Carl knew well, he would turn away, go back into his camp, and slam the door.

"There was a time in his life when he was no pussycat," said George Mattor. "I remember a fellow who was digging gold near the camp and Carl went back and got his shotgun. 'You get the hell out of there or I'll shoot!' Anyone who got the impression that they could take advantage of him was in for a big surprise. Carl was his own man."

He had reason for distrusting people. One late September, a couple came to see him. The man said he was a taxi driver from Rumford. Would Carl take him out panning? The woman wasn't interested in mining and remained at the camp. Carl showed the man what to do and ran a few demonstration pans. When they got back, the woman seemed in a hurry to leave. Carl got suspicious and looked behind a picture where he had taped a vial of gold. The vial was gone. He grabbed his shotgun and ran up the trail, but the two were just driving away by the bridge as Carl caught sight of them.

Yet there were many good times with entire families who came and spent the day on the river. D. Priscilla Higgins of Lisbon Falls, Maine, remembered how she and her first husband, Kenneth Carl, and their two children would bring the food and they would cook dinner for them all. Mrs. Higgins said Carl didn't smile much, and she recalled how angry he got at a man who came down and wanted to bulldoze the bank in front of Carl's camp. "I got no time for you!" said Carl, turning his back and walking away. She spoke of the concentrates he kept in his camp. There was a huge amount of gold in the black sand. Also one day, Mrs. Higgins' younger sister, a girl around puberty, got into her swimsuit and left her bra outside her knapsack in front of the camp. Carl came by and picking up the bra, holding it like a dead fish, walked over to the family, and with noticeable irritation in his voice, said: "Whose riggin is this!"

Suddenly, for no known reason, Carl wanted nothing to do with his friends. One day, Esther and Lee Knapp went down, and Carl refused to come out of the camp. The Knapps, who had always gone out of their way to do things for him, couldn't understand why he was behaving this way with them. Finally, Lee Knapp walked into the camp and asked: "Carl, what in the hell is the matter?" And his reply was: "I don't trust nobody."

But these black moods would leave him. Carrie Bristol recalled a day when she and her son and daughter-in-law had Carl show them how to pan. Later Mrs. Bristol's son drove Carl into Rumford to shop while the two women spent the afternoon digging for gold. Carl didn't stop talking all the way into town and back.

He liked being with young people, and most of the parents who took their children down the East Branch to meet "the old German hermit" were surprised how well he and young people got along. They needn't have been. Carl had an honest, direct way of talking with them, and they respected him. This was obvious to Clarence Bateman when Carl went on field trips with the boys from Camp Kawanhee. Dean and Ann McCrillis recalled how Carl would walk all the way from Byron Corner to the store in Roxbury to buy ice cream for their two boys. Mrs. McCrillis would give them spoons and the three would sit on the front steps until the half gallon container was empty.

If Carl got the idea he had been slighted or misused, he would carry a grudge for days. Then he would start talking as if nothing had happened. It didn't take much to provoke him. Stanley Voter recalled going mining with a friend, and in the woods Voter found a rusty crowbar sticking in the ground. He pulled the bar out, and his friend was using it as Carl came along. Carl took one look and grabbed the crowbar. "That's mine, you goddamned thieves!" He blamed Voter's friend for stealing it and went up river clutching the bar.

"I remember when Shilling broke his leg," said Rodney Davis. "I think it was George Mattor who found him. Carl had snapped his ankle on a rock and it was wintertime and he had burned all his furniture in the camp trying to keep warm. That may have turned him around in his need to see more people. But his attitude was often hostile. If he wanted to see you, he would wave you down. If not, he would go into his camp and get his shotgun and nose around and say nothing. It was then you knew that Carl wasn't in the mood for anybody."

George Mattor felt that Carl had "a lot of fair-weathered friends." Many of them showered him with gifts and brought in beer. But they never got ahead of Carl by praising him or giving him things. "A lot of people would go up there and sweet-talk him," said Helen Barker. "He was quite a man because he could see right through that kind of person."

Those who went down the trail and got to know Carl soon realized that here was a man who did indeed like his beer. His favorite was Budweiser, but anything that had an alcoholic content was appreciated. His eyes would light up when people came with a bottle.

George Mattor would sometimes tease Carl a little.

"He'd come to my house and I had a morris chair beside the door as you go in and he'd always sit there. Usually, I'd offer him a beer in the summertime. But sometimes I wouldn't offer him one. It was then he'd start teetering and squirming. Finally, he'd say: 'What's the matter? Haven't you got any beer?' "

"He also loved German beer," said Carrie Bristol. "We went up once with groceries on our snowmobiles, and it was about time for the river to go out. 'Oh,' he said, 'I wish I had known that you were coming. I'd have had you brought me some German beer. It would have tasted so very good.' " On their way home, Mrs. Bristol and her daughter decided they would chance crossing the river again on their snowmobiles. They went to Roxbury and bought two cases of German beer and took them down to Carl. "That old man was so happy," remembered Mrs. Bristol. "You'd have thought we had given him a million dollars."

Carl was a handsome man in his early forties when he came to Byron, and several women in town were interested in him. But he didn't seem to notice. Romance wasn't on his mind. Even when he boarded in one of the Byron homes where several attractive daughters laughed and flirted, Carl never gave the girls' parents any reason for concern. Not once, in all the long talks he had with male friends at his camp, did he speak of women or marriage. Perhaps Carl got hurt badly, more than he wanted to admit, and this was why he never spoke of that time in the 1950s when there had been someone in his life.

She was a woman in her late thirties or early forties, from Cape Cod, and they met on the river. Dean McCrillis remembered letting her stay in one of his houses in Byron. Carl had fallen in love with her, and he claimed that they were going to get married. But the woman's fifteen-year-old son didn't want his mother living downriver with Carl and was determined to do whatever he could to break them up.

She came a second time to Byron, and between visits there were many letters. McCrillis had to take the mail all the way up to the corner so Carl could get it quickly. But that wasn't all. Carl came down and got Mrs. McCrillis to answer the letters for him. It was a busy time for everyone. They were to be married in two or three days, but the letters stopped. Carl kept to himself on the river, and for a time he was in a dark and ugly mood.

"When Carl talked to a woman," said Ann McCrillis, "he never looked at her. He always kept his eyes averted. He'd only look up once in a while, and he knew us very well."

When digging along the East Branch, Carl used a ten-foot sluice, and in the early sixties he got a gasoline motor and pump which increased the amount of overburden he could go through in a day. There wasn't a man on the river who worked harder than Carl, and this was one reason why he came up with more gold. But he also studied the river. He kept his eye on boulders along the banks and measured them each year to see how much they had shifted in the spring flood. One particular boulder interested him. "I have been watching that rock now for six years," he told George Mattor, "and it's been moving every year in the spring. Last year it moved two inches."

George Mattor enjoyed watching his friend hopping from stone to stone. Carl was like a mountain goat, and he never wore waders. On one occasion, Carl, who was well into his eighties at the time and more than a generation older, offered to help Mattor across the river. Carl's red bandanna and battered hat were familiar sights along the banks. He cut his hair in the spring and fall, wore long-johns all summer, and when he had to read something, he pulled out a pair of glasses that had been patched many times.

"It's in the muck, in the muck," he would tell Charlie Damery as they worked with full buckets and dumped pail after pail into Carl's sluice. "And you've got to break rock." When Charlie made himself a rocker, Carl told him to knock one end out and use it as a sluice. Such gadgetry was useless. "That's no good to find gold," declared Carl.

When greenhorns or friends went sluicing with him, they were all expected to work. "Shuffle, shuffle," Lee Knapp recalls Carl telling the crew when they weren't shovelling fast enough to suit him. And Esther Knapp remembers that she was the only woman Carl would allow to pick rocks from the sluice. He would tell the other women: "You keep hands out!"

Carl Shilling and Crew Courtesy of Arnold Howe

Carl could run a pan faster than anyone on the Swift and work more clay through his sluice. "I think over the years he learned more about that river than we will ever know," said Harvey Packard, a Dixfield, Maine miner who has found several nuggets on the East Branch. "He learned how the gold got there and where it came from. If Carl Shilling were alive right now, he could get an ounce a week."

Carl never saved his gold. He sold it to meet living expenses, and there were several people who bought his findings. The two most frequent purchasers were Carl Jarvis from Connecticut and Dean McCrillis. There were several big nuggets that Carl found during his forty years on the Swift River. One piece weighed more than an ounce and was shaped like the boot of Italy, and another had a piece of quartz embedded like a crown.

George Mattor (left) and Carl Shilling Courtesy of William Mattor

Stories about Carl's gold are still being told, and the nuggets get bigger and bigger. People tell of seeing two half gallon milk bottles of gold that he kept under the floor in his bedroom—that would be more than a person could lift.

A lot of the gold that Carl found was taken in front of his camp —the site of the old placer. But for several years he was reluctant to dig there because it would wreck his garden. Finally, he changed his mind and decided that it would be worthwhile to reach bedrock. One whole summer, when panners came and wondered where they should work, Carl told them: "You come right here! On my place!"

"They'd dig like badgers in there," said George Mattor. "He was just letting them help him. One day I was standing there talking with Carl when he had two or three digging, and someone dug up an old cooking spoon. I said: 'Carl, I thought you said it hadn't been dug before?' And Carl started giggling: 'Hee, hee, hee!' He just wanted them to get rid of the overburden."

When Carl reached retirement age, Clarence Bateman contacted Dean McCrillis' father, a lawyer, and a benefit of social security was worked out. It's still a mystery how Carl's application was approved—he wasn't an American citizen. McCrillis remembered his father working on the papers.

The land on which Carl built his camp belonged to Stowell and McGregor, a woodworking concern in Dixfield, which was later part of Timberland Corporation. Carl was given permission to use the land lease free. But he was subject to town taxes for his building. One year he decided to build a small addition and with revaluation his taxes increased six dollars.

Clarence Young, who was a selectman at the time, went down with his grandson, Dean McCrillis, to talk with Carl. But there was no reasoning with him, no more than when the radio had been the problem. McCrillis remembered his grandfather being terribly upset.

Carl went into Rumford and bought a wall tent that had a small screened porch. It didn't have a floor, and it was wintertime, but this made no difference to a man who was angry with town officials. They wouldn't get six more dollars from him!

He tore part of his camp down, boarded up the windows, and moved into the tent. He made a wooden bed for his mattress and sleeping bag and put in a small stove. Concerned friends wondered how an eighty-three-year-old man kept from freezing when the temperature dropped below zero.

His anger only increased when someone paid the taxes for him. After all the unfairness from the Town of Byron, he complained, now people were stealing his home.

"Carl," several tried to reason with him, "no harm is meant." But he didn't believe them. "I don't trust nobody," he replied.

"When he rebuilt his camp and moved back in," said George Mattor, "it never looked quite as quaint." Yet Carl was satisfied. He had made a stand, and the selectmen now knew how he felt about more taxes.

Ellis Quinn went down to see him one winter day with a jug of applejack. There was more than three feet of snow on the ground, and Quinn had on snowshoes. As he neared the camp, he suddenly heard Carl shout from high on the hill above the trail. His friend was waist-deep in snow with an axe in one hand and a log on his shoulder. Quinn stood waiting while Carl waded down. Once on the trail, Carl dropped the log, and the two men stood talking for several minutes. Then Carl asked his visitor if he wanted coffee. Quinn accepted and offered to carry the log. "He said I could, and he just walked away. It was a piece of hardwood, and I had all I could do to pick it up. I struggled down to his camp with it and dropped it on the ground. That man had carried it off the mountain without snowshoes."

Someone talked Carl into burning gas one year. He wouldn't have to cut so much wood, and it was a convenience. So Carl had a large cylinder brought in and a good used stove installed. But the arrangement didn't work right. Carl lost his temper and he threw both stove and cylinder over the bank into the river.

"He stood only a little more than five feet," said Ellis Quinn, "but in my opinion he was a giant of a man." Then Quinn remembered a rock that Carl wanted to move away from the camp. The boulder was at least eight feet long and six feet wide. When Quinn came back a month later, the rock had been moved. "It was fifty yards from where it was, and nobody had helped him."

Carl never trusted doctors, and the hospital was the last place on earth for him, but he had to go there when he scalded his foot with a kettle of hot water. The burn got infected when he tried to treat it himself. Finally, realizing that he had to have help, he wrapped rags around his foot and walked up the railroad bed to the bridge and then over Dingle Hill to the village. It was more than three miles in the snow. If there had not been a snowmobile trail, he wouldn't have made it. Carl never got over how much it cost him for his stay in the hospital.

Esther Knapp baked a cake for Carl on his 80th birthday, and a photograph of the occasion was taken. Esther was one of the few people he trusted completely. Carl wanted the picture and got it. He said the photograph would be in the book he was going to write.

The idea of writing a book about his life and the search for gold wouldn't have occurred to Carl during his early years on the river. But the more people visited him and asked questions and his reputation increased, the more seriously he thought about a book. He even had a title. It would be called "Tumbledown Gold." He had long given up the theory that the source of gold on the East Branch was from Tumbledown Mountain—he was convinced that the gold was glacial and from Canada—but the title was a good one, he told Carrie Bristol.

"Carl asked my daughter, Diane, if she had a typewriter and could type," recalled Mrs. Bristol, "and when she said she did, Carl said: 'Then you will be the one to help write my book about Tumbledown Gold.' He would always bring up the idea of the book, but he never got to the point of doing anything about it."

George Mattor claimed that Carl was writing it. But no manuscript was found in Carl's belongings. He and Diane Bristol never got together, and if there was a collaborator, that person was never identified. Lenna Young, in her article about Carl in *Maine Life,* after Shilling's death, was able to provide some details that Carl must have recorded, but most of Mrs. Young's article was from her own point of view. "He wanted someone else to do it because he couldn't write it himself," said Mrs. Young's daughter, Irene Hutchinson.

Stanley Voter, who visited Carl from time to time, believed that money was the reason why the book never got under way. "I don't know who had been talking to Carl about this, but somebody put the bug in his ear that he get it in writing and get the money before telling the story. I think there was a third party involved."

Carl's decision to buy an 8 mm camera may have had something to do with the book. Perhaps he felt that films of him and others on the river would be good promotional material. Carl wasn't a cameraman—his hands shook and his pictures were out of focus—but he did try to include a variety of things: river views, birds and squirrels, even Christmas ornaments on a tree in his yard one December. There were shots of Carl and his friends using a come-along to move a boulder and of a crew hosing a bank in order to catch flakes of gold at the bottom of rivulets. The most memorable footage included Lee and Esther Knapp and Irene Provencher. They were all on snowmobiles. The Knapps remembered how much Carl enjoyed staging the scene: Carl falls off the back of a snowmobile, rolls in the snow, gets up, wades hip high to the trail, and slumps into the drifts again. A remarkable feat for a man well into his eighties. Edwin Provencher shot the scene.

Eventually, Carl got tired of taking pictures and sold the camera. After his death, Lenna Young donated the films to Gould Academy, and a teacher ran a few reels but decided that they were of no interest. The films were about to be destroyed when someone at the school learned that George Mattor had been a friend of Carl's. Mattor now has a shoe box full of 8 mm reels.

"We tried to borrow a Super 8 projector from a man up the road," said Carrie Bristol. "Carl came down one night all prepared to see them. He was so thrilled. We waited for a couple of hours before the man showed up, and he didn't have the right projector. It was after dark when Carl started up the trail. I know he was terribly disappointed."

Carl hadn't been himself for some weeks, and one day when Mattor brought down a bag of sugar for some strawberries that Carl was going to preserve, Mattor sensed that something was wrong. His friend wouldn't admit that he was feeling poorly; he only said: "Why don't you come every couple of days and check on me?"

Then on July 4, 1977, Mattor and two acquaintances walked down to Carl's. They found him unconscious, half on the mattress and half on the floor. There were no windows open, and the camp was stifling. One of them hurried back up the trail for help while Mattor and the other man tried to make Carl comfortable.

"He was in horrible shape," recalled Mattor. "His lips were dry, and he looked like somebody who had been in the desert. We got some water from the river and a towel and I wiped his mouth. I asked 'Does that feel better, Carl?' And he said: 'Yah!' That was the last thing he ever said."

Even while the two men were with Carl and waiting for the rescue service, the search for a dying man's treasures had begun. "Carl was on the mattress on the floor," said Mattor, "and I was holding his head. This guy came busting in and started going around the camp, saying: 'Hey, where's the gold? Where's the gold?' And I said: 'What are you talking about?' He said: 'Let's find the gold!' I told that guy: 'You better get out of here right now!' "

Under Carl's pillow, Mattor found a wallet with more than eight hundred dollars. After Carl had been taken to the hospital, the three who found him went to Mattor's house, counted the bills, signed a statement verifying the amount, took the cash to a bank in Rumford, and deposited it. But some people in Byron weren't happy.

"I got accused of taking half of the money," said Mattor with a scowl. "But I just took it from whence it came. They were down there at Carl's like a bunch of wolves opening the gate to the lambs' pen."

Carl Shilling died in the hospital on July 18th without regaining consciousness. During the time he was in the hospital, the floorboards of his camp were being pried loose. One looter went down on his motorcycle, and Mattor saw the tracks. All that night, George Mattor sat on the bank behind Carl's camp waiting with a gun. But nobody came.

The root cellar was quickly dug up, and metal detectors were brought in to locate the jars of nuggets that some believed were buried nearby. Everything was turned over or broken into. The bird feeder lines were pulled and vegetables sacked up the trail. One person proudly admitted that he had potatoes from that last garden, but Carl never raised potatoes. Cars would stop on Dingle Hill, in Ellis Quinn's driveway across the road from Mattor's place, and when George went out to see what was wanted, the drivers would be looking for the road to Carl's. "We're old, old friends!" they would say. "You're no friends," Mattor would tell them. "Get out!"

Gold hunters were staying down at Carl's for days at a time, and the selectmen became concerned. Fires were kindled at night and left unattended. Timberland was contacted, and it was agreed that the Town of Byron would make arrangements to burn what was left of the camp.

Two decades have gone by since Carl's death, but the howl of metal detectors can still be heard on some summer days. There are few things left on the site—only an old bedspring and bits of rusting metal. But one gold miner is convinced that the ghost of Carl Shilling still inhabits the place. He is sure that he heard Carl's footsteps around his tent late one night when camping there.

Carl had once written some verses in German for Lenna Young. He told her that they were on his school diploma and he had memorized them. Mrs. Young said that his writing "was clear and in a very fancy scroll." She had the verses translated and found that they were from the Bible, in the Gospel of John. "Then spoke Jesus again unto them, saying, 'I am the light of the world; he that followeth me shall not walk in darkness, but shall have the light of life.' " Mrs. Young had the minister read these at Carl's funeral.

Carl Shilling had his own lifestyle, and he wasn't the kind of person to be influenced by others. Difficult as he could be at times, his friends were loyal. Though he kept to himself most of his life, he never lost contact with the outside world. People came to him. Like Perley Whitney, he, too, is a legend. But for those who got to know Carl, he became more real with the passing years. What kind of a man was he? Most of his friends, when asked the question, smile and reply: "Carl was Carl."

The Summer of Yellow Rocks

"How did you two get interested in prospecting?" The question often is asked at our *Maine Gold* booth. I know that people are curious about us and our mining, but half the time I get the feeling that they are wondering if this might be something for them. There is an excitement in gold hunting, and every time we go on the river the adventure is different. We no longer care if we find gold or come home empty-handed. It's the thrill of being out. Even as a child, when I pretended that every white pebble in our brook was a nugget, I knew the fun of playing the game was in the looking.

We had been on a couple of gold hunts before Stella and I began searching the Maine rivers for signs of color. I remember a day trip into the Superstition Mountains in Arizona with friends to search for the Lost Dutchman's Mine, and one summer, when we were living in Ireland, Stella and I joined a dig with several people who hoped to unearth a chest of gold ingots buried in a field behind an old monastery.

Stella is the treasure hunter. She is always finding pennies and dimes on the ground, and I am the kind of person who goes around stepping on them. But we both became interested in gold prospecting through metal detecting. The idea of looking for andirons and candlesticks around old foundations was appealing at first, but I soon decided this kind of treasure hunting wasn't for me. I often found myself surrounded by poison ivy, and I kept seeing Stella at the bottom of some deep well. Then I read a book called *Electronic Prospecting* by Charles Garrett, Bob Grant, and Roy Lagal. Immediately, I was bitten by the gold bug, and my fever raged out of control. Stella and I soon had two green "Gravity Trap" plastic gold pans, and we were scouring the banks with our detectors.

It is nearly impossible to find a nugget on a Maine river with metal detectors. Since gold works its way to the bottom of crevices and usually is covered with considerable overburden, it is beyond the range of most detectors. Metal detectors are useful in locating black sand, and where there is a concentration of this heavy magnetic iron, there is a better chance of finding gold. Whenever I see a person scrambling around with a shovel, plastic gold pan, and a detector, I remember our first full season of prospecting. I call it the summer of yellow rocks.

One day during that first year, I took a friend gold hunting on the Sandy River in Avon, between Phillips and Strong. This is where the stream is slow-moving and has a heavier overburden. One would have to dig ten or twenty feet in this area to reach bedrock. But I wasn't easily discouraged, and to be honest, I then thought of myself as quite an expert. "We'll dig right here," I told him as a full spade of sandy gravel was taken from the top at the edge of the river and thrown into the plastic plan. "We should find plenty of good gold here!"

"You see that?" I asked, holding up a white pebble with threads of yellow discoloration. "That's it!" My friend peered at the stone skeptically. After I ran the pan and gave him a rather complicated panning lesson that I had memorized from a book on mining, we went nugget hunting along the bank with detectors.

I don't know why so many beginners think that every yellow rock on a stream is a gold nugget. I blush when I think of our first season. We went out every weekend, all summer long, and never found a trace of color. But we didn't keep all the hard luck to ourselves. A year or two ago, I met a beginner on the river who was having his share.

I was near Carl's old campsite panning one afternoon when I felt someone behind me, turned, and saw a man in hip waders who was carrying a knapsack. He could have been a fisherman until I saw the spade.

"You having any luck?" he asked.

I told him that I had found only a few flakes, and I showed him my vial.

He took the tiny bottle, shook it, and peered at the particles of color.

"That ain't very much," he said.

"I guess I'm not going to get rich on it," I agreed, taking the vial back and stuffing it into my shirt pocket. "Are you getting any gold?"

"Oh, I got a mayonnaise jar partly-filled," he replied.

"You got a what!"

"A jar partly-filled," he repeated in a casual sort of way.

"You mind showing me?"

The man slid out of his knapsack and brought out a medium-sized jar half-filled with the nicest yellow pebbles that the East Branch of the Swift River could provide.

I hesitated, wondering if I should say something. Then it came to me that the stranger was feeling sorry for my poor showing. His pity was more than I could stand.

"Mister," I told him, "what you have there isn't gold. Those are yellow rocks!"

He looked at them briefly, carefully put the jar back into his knapsack, and said no more. I got the feeling that he thought I was a poor loser.

I went back to the stream, ran another pan, and when I looked up again he was gone.

Today, A Hundred Pieces of Gold

Bill Garrett of Chelsea, Maine was the one who showed Stella and me how to use a gold pan. We were out nugget hunting with our metal detectors on the East Branch when a man stopped to talk with us. He smiled and asked if we were finding gold. I dodged the question by saying that we had just got there. Bill reached into a trouser pocket, pulled out a jewelry box, and snapped open the lid. There were three partly-filled two ounce vials of Maine gold. We quickly put down our detectors and Bill Garrett gave us a panning lesson.

We were the first to hire him. I offered Bill twenty dollars for a day of instructions. I think it was then that he decided to teach gold panning as a way of earning extra money. Over a period of several years, Bill Garrett taught hundreds who came from all over the country, and he also held summer mining classes on the Swift for the University of Maine at Augusta.

Stella got a tiny piece of gold the day we went out with Garrett, but I found nothing. I panned a few flakes the next weekend on a ledge by the Sandy River above Phillips. The thrill of seeing that first bit of color has only been equaled on one occasion—the time I got my $1,000 nugget. I remember holding my breath as I put those first glittering specks into a vial filled with water. A strip of black electrician's tape on one side of the bottle showed off the gold strikingly. We tented every weekend at Mount Blue State Park, and we dug and panned below the site on the East Branch where Bill ran his pump and sluice. We had a way of counting our successes that second summer. When we got back to camp or home, we would tell ourselves and others: "Today we got a hundred pieces of gold, and yesterday we did even better! A hundred and seven pieces to be exact!" We counted every flake we found, and there was a new vial for every outing on the river.

We didn't realize it, but we were falling into a trap. We were allowing the sight of gold in our pans to blind our common sense; the more color we found, the more frantically we dug behind rocks and into crevices. We didn't even stop long enough to enjoy our lunch. All day in the blistering sun, we worked like chain gang prisoners. I still remember the beatings I took on the river that year. I was covered with insect bites, my hands were battered, the muscles in my back pulled, and I went through three pairs of waders within two months. In addition to the frantic way we worked, a senseless routine was soon established. We would drive over the back road to Byron, past Tumbledown Mountain, at dawn in order to get to our favorite spot before anyone else. If we didn't get there first, we knew that our whole day would be ruined. Some days we dug for more than ten hours and it made little difference to us if it was pouring rain or one of the hottest days of the year.

That back road from Weld to Byron, twisting up and down hills for eight miles through the woods, was then an obstacle course. It was narrow with few turnouts, and there were jagged boulders sticking up in the middle of the traveled way. I had the worst possible vehicle for such a terrain. It was a huge sedan painted bright yellow for the lemon it was, and the distance between the muffler and the ground wasn't high enough for a cat to crawl under. My garageman kept saying: "You're scraping the bejesus out of it!" But going that way was a shortcut and it gave us more time for panning .

Financially that summer, we gained nothing. Garage bills, gas and oil, bottles of insect repellent and sunscreen, waders, raincoats, vials, bandaids, park fees, and a new transmission were just a few expenses. There was also the time spent panning—probably four or five hundred hours. All this for less than an ounce of gold!

I wouldn't do it again, even if a mother lode were under my feet. When one becomes so obsessed that there is no joy and only frenzy, it is time to give a thing up. We were blinded, sick with the fever that so many beginning prospectors get, and we were no longer capable of feeling fortunate for having found an activity that we could enjoy together. When the water became so cold that our hands began to ache, we stopped going to the Swift. It was then we saw the foolishness of listing our flakes instead of counting our pleasures.

Two Kinds of Fever

Prospectors come down with two kinds of fever. There is gold, and then there is that less pleasant affliction known as cabin fever. I was feeling isolated and at loose ends from February to April before our third year of gold hunting. The mercury stayed at the bottom of the thermometer like gold in a crevice, and the snow drifted its overburden into the dooryard. I went about my life as best I could, but part of me was back on the river.

Sometimes, in the late evening, I would spread my geological survey maps on the kitchen table and take imaginary prospecting trips up streams and tributaries. When I got tired of this kind of hunting I would leaf through the mining catalogs and think of new pry bars, wedges, and crevicing tools. Was it time for me to treat myself to a folding mattock? Then I would step out on the porch to see how much snow had fallen since dinnertime.

"If you keep looking for gold," said a neighbor one day when I had exhausted the subject of prospecting, "you may well end up a millionaire."

"I'm already a millionaire," I told him, "because I've found something I really like doing."

What I said sounded good to me then, and I can still see some wisdom in the remark, but I wasn't being completely honest. I think my attitude was still wrong. There are those sensible people who look upon gold hunting as a recreational pastime; a hobby that gets one out of the house and into nature. I was allowing it to interfere with my life and to crowd my priorities. I knew it was a mistake to count every grain of color and to punish myself in my quest to find more. I had made up my mind that this wasn't going to happen during our third year of mining.

"Never mind how many flakes we find," I said to Stella one afternoon when patches of bare ground could be seen on the lawn. "I think we should look around for bigger gold."

I had read an article on the possibility of a mother lode near Stratton, Maine, and since we had spent many hours on streams in the area with our detectors, I thought it would be a good location to begin the season. So many Maine prospectors once they start going to the Swift River end up there for good. I didn't want us to get into a routine and narrow our opportunities. Gone were the days when a Carl Shilling or Perley Whitney could get several ounces from a watershed crevice along the East Branch. There were now other places just as promising.

When all the snow had melted, finally, and the spring floods had subsided, we began prospecting in the Carrabassett Valley, above

Kingfield, and near Mount Bigelow. We cleaned crevices to see if we could determine the direction of the gold. Unlike the Swift, the Carrabassett River has finer and more widely scattered flakes. We soon found there wasn't enough color around Bigelow to establish direction. But we kept going back. What interested us was the black sand—never had I seen coarser and darker iron magnetite. Swift River concentrates have a high garnet content which leaves a reddish tinge. I mistakenly thought that we would locate more gold as the sands got blacker. But like all rivers, the Carrabassett is whimsical and unpredictable and never willing to reveal its secrets.

The South Branch, the stream on the right where the road goes to Sugarloaf, surprised us. It looked so unpromising as we put on our hip waders and shouldered our gear. We nearly broke our necks getting in there—I have never seen such slippery rocks! Between two boulders the size of elephants, we came across a pool lined with clay. When we scooped some of this material from the bottom of the stream and panned it, we found a night sky of tiny gold flakes in our pans. I don't know why we never went back to inspect the area more closely. I guess one of the problems of prospecting in Maine is that there are so many places where gold can be found. As I write this, with a dozen other brooks on our list, I'm promising myself another trip in there. This time we'll take a shortcut through the woods to the pool. Rock hounds would find the South Branch worth exploring for its green jasper.

By mid-summer, we had moved further north into the Coburn Gore district and the wilderness tracts east of Eustis, Maine. Gold Brook and Kibby Stream are two waters that keep crevices well supplied with run-off gold. I found this out when I opened a crevice I had cleaned the previous year. Somewhere in this vicinity, I think there is an outcropping or lode of gold with commercial potential.

The South Branch of Dead River, along the road between Rangeley and Stratton, also proved productive. Within sight of the highway we found several spots where the panning was excellent. I know this stream has been overlooked. When I think of the centuries that gold has been drifting down and lining the crevices, I get excited.

Nile Brook in Rangeley still exasperates me. It's less than three miles long, and from a clay bank, or near it, there seems to come a never-ending supply of gold. I'm not the only one who is convinced that there is something unusual happening here. Prospectors have been drawn to the brook for more than a hundred years. On our first trip there, Stella panned a tiny piece that was both platinum and gold. Considering how frequently this short run of water has been worked the amount of gold recovered could well exceed most rivers in Maine. I always like to go there during the spring floods and stand at the bridge on Route 4. There is a lot of water coming down that hillside and with it a churning mass of debris.

As much as we enjoyed prospecting for bigger gold and getting acquainted with other streams in Franklin, Oxford, and Somerset counties, we occasionally went back to the East Branch of the Swift for a day of panning. Though we still liked seeing those flakes on a background of black tape in our water-filled vials, we now had time, or thought we had, to notice the waters rushing past us and the patterns of light on the ground under the trees.

Then one early September day, probably the Labor Day weekend, everything changed for us again. I came down with another case of gold fever, this one even more severe. It all happened when we walked down the old railroad bed below Carl's and met a man and his dog. There is no prospector around more enthusiastic about mining than Harvey Packard. Stella and I have gone digging several times with him, and on a few of these outings we have found nuggets weighing more than a pennyweight. Harvey doesn't mind sharing with others. That is, if they can keep up with him as he runs down the trail to his favorite place below Carl's. It was in this location that we came across him and his dog, Teddy. Harvey was working his sluice as we waded across the river. "You dig right there," he told us. "A fellow from Rumford found a lot of gold in that spot just last week."

During the next six weeks, until the waters nearly froze our hands, we dug for gold and bruised ourselves on boulders that were in our way. We were on that inside bend of the river every weekend, and I would drive over to Byron from Mount Vernon at least twice a week while Stella was at work in Augusta. This time, luck was with us. In a month and a half, we found an ounce of fine gold and five nuggets. Two of these nuggets were two pennyweights, the width of my little fingernail, and the others were only slightly smaller. It didn't take long for the rumors to circulate that we had struck pay dirt. It seemed that every time I found a nugget, someone was passing by as I panned it. Some of the miners wildly exaggerated our finds. They said we were finding nuggets that weighed several ounces. One day, when I stopped to visit a camp owner on the mountain in Byron, he asked me quite seriously if we had found a pound of gold that fall. It took me several moments before I could answer. I think my hesitation convinced him that we were now rich.

It was at this time that we turned in our sedan for a new pickup truck. Now, rumors were adrift on the river. "They paid for that pickup with the gold they found below Carl's," a miner told Bill Garrett. Bill, who knew all about our activities, assured the man that it wasn't true. "These folks aren't living in Alaska or California," said Bill. "This is the state of Maine, in Oxford County!"

The season was definitely over that late October afternoon when we waded across the East Branch to the landing at the end of Bateman's Lane. I was thinking how slowly time would pass before I could get back on the river. As I started the truck to drive home, I knew I had both kinds of fever, and it wasn't even winter.

Maine's Mining Boom and Bust

The man who shouted "There's gold at Sutter's Mill" and alerted

San Francisco was Sam Brennan of Saco, Maine. Brennan's cry reached Maine newspapers in September 1848, and within the next 12 months some 67 ships sailed from Portland, Bangor, Belfast, and Eastport by the way of Cape Horn to join the forty-niners.

Most of those who went could have stayed at home for all the precious metal they found. Though gold fever never reached the frenzied peak that it did in California, Maine had its own rush of gold and silver. This was due partly to colorful promoters of worthless stock, and dreamers who allowed their hopes to overshadow reality.

The first to have faith in the mining future of Maine was Frank L. Bartlett, a state assayer. Bartlett believed that the governor and his council repressed the truth about Maine's mining potential for fear that such news would retard agriculture.

Frank L. Bartlett, 1879

"A damnable bill of nonsense!" shouted one council member at an Augusta hearing. But news of Maine's first gold strike at Madrid in 1854 spread rapidly. Perhaps Bartlett was right after all. "It is a singular fact," said Bartlett in 1877, at the time that some out-of-staters found gold and silver in Acton, Maine, "that the finding of traces of gold should inspire men with wild hopes of rich discoveries." Within a few years, the Acton Silver Mine was reported to be the richest in New England. One shaft was sunk 140 feet, and a tunnel was cut 115 feet into a hillside. In some places, even at the shallow depth of 19 feet, the mine yielded as much as 300 ounces of silver per ton of ore.

Bartlett, realizing that this was the time to change the minds of the state bureaucracy and others who had little faith in Maine as a gold and silver state, quickly produced two books. *The Minerals of New England,* 1877, and *The Mines of Maine,* 1879.

"The industry now attracts unusual attention," wrote Bartlett "and it is destined to increase until the tide of emigration turns this way; it will give employment to the masses; it will give fortunes to some; to have a piece of Maine mining stock in one's pocket will prove a considerable financial consolation."

In vain Bartlett warned farmers against investing their capital in mining stock. He felt that it should be left to the capitalists who could better afford to risk their money. The warning also was completely ignored by hundreds of small-businessmen who could ill afford speculating in Maine gold and silver.

During the same year that Frank Bartlett published his *The Mines of Maine,* the mining industry got its biggest boost. Willam Morris Stewart, a former senator from Nevada and a friend of miners all over the country since his own days as a forty-niner, visited Blue Hill, Maine in December 1897.

Recent assays had established the presence of gold and silver in ore taken at the Douglass Copper Mine, and Stewart was impressed. "There is possibly no spot on this planet where mining can be more expeditiously carried forward," he told reporters. The town had a good harbor, high quality ore, and timber for mine construction. Stewart was convinced that Maine mines had operational advantages over those in the West.

Newspapers along the entire East Coast accepted Stewart's opinion as fact, and even the *New York Tribune* declared that if such veins had been discovered in remote regions of Colorado, entire settlements with several thousand inhabitants would already have been established.

Money poured into Maine. Even those who had their doubts were eager to invest. With thermometers at zero and the snow drifting, men were out prospecting in their pastures. At Isle au Haut, Maine, every man and boy "had his pockets full of rocks," and more than half the women of Round Island spent their days looking for precious metals. All over the state, property owners were drilling and blasting ledges without waiting for an assay. Companies were quickly formed and stocks printed: Lewiston had three exchanges where mining stocks were bought and sold, and the biggest exchange in the state was established almost overnight in Bangor.

Yet there were skeptics. The *Maine Mining Journal* repeatedly warned its readers against speculation, and Professor Young, a voice in mining affairs at Bowdoin College, insisted that nine out of ten mining companies were "unmitigated, irresponsible swindlers." But the mines kept opening. Two months after Stewart's arrival in Maine, 600 men were working at Blue Hill, 1,000 in Sullivan, and 550 in Acton. Most of these miners were farmers and fishermen.

There were management problems. William Darling was dissatisfied with his City of Boston Mine in Blue Hill, and acting on Stewart's recommendations, Darling hired a superintendent from the Comstock Silver and Gold Mine in Nevada in 1879. One superintendent followed another in rapid succession. Even though these experts weren't in Blue Hill for long, they did change the looks of things. Large and elegant buildings, like those erected at the Comstock Mine, rose within weeks. The Twin Lead Mine had a four-gable hip roof on its shaft house with a cupola "surmounted by a weather vane consisting of a handsome game cock." The Milton Mine at Sullivan was even gaudier. In the cupola of the hoisting works was a huge lantern, 36 feet above the ocean and visible for miles. Over shaft Number 2, bathrooms were installed with the latest fixtures. But worse for the stockholders, long before these building were completed the superintendents had bought unnecessary machinery, such as costly stamping mills, furnaces, and giant steam engines.

Older mines which had operated successfully on limited budgets began to expand. Blue Hill Copper Mine ordered diamond drills and hoisting machinery capable of 800 feet, although its shafts were only a fraction of that depth. In addition to these expenses, the company built the largest concentrating plant on the continent, a three-story unit covering more than 3,000 square feet.

Mining towns all over the state were becoming crowded. People from all levels of life rushed to Maine, from as far away as Wales, Scotland, and Sweden. And as always, in every mining boom, there were the swindlers selling stocks. People bought blindly, hopeful of profit. Worried by the rampant speculation, the *Maine Mining Journal* warned against "companies that organize, sell stock and endeavor to find a mine afterwards." But the fever continued. By April 1880, 123 companies existed in Maine, and Blue Hill alone had 39 of them.

New stores, houses, and stables were built as the quiet seacoast communities became roaring towns. Colonel William Darling—mine owners were often called Colonel, General, or Professor during the boom—announced that he would erect two large blocks in Blue Hill and "an elegant and spacious hotel with a capacity of 75 rooms." But this wasn't to be. In April 1880 came the beginning of a nationwide depression. Stocks fell and mining stocks plunged. Colonel Darling closed his exchange and withdrew from active life "because of the severity of his rheumatism." The *Boston Herald* assessed the situation and came to a conclusion:

"People of Maine have this spring made a most valuable discovery. They have found that a hole in the ground is not a mine; that a man who can dig a well or blast a ledge...is not a miner; that assays are deceptive and skilled miners from California pan out no better than assays. They have found that mining is a business and not fun, that it requires capital, experience and time before results are reached....Now let Maine miners take courage and go ahead."

But going ahead was difficult. People were now suspicious of mining stocks, and the companies had dangerously overexpanded. Then the price of ore rose and prospects seemed brighter. Colonel

Darling's rheumatism improved. He still owned his mansion, a huge diamond ring, and he had one active mine, called the Favorite.

Maine Mining Stock

Problems still beset the industry. Many of the mines flooded, especially those in Sullivan which were close to the sea. Pumping was unsatisfactory, and some mines could only operate when the tide was out. Since Maine workers objected to Sunday employment, the shafts were partly filled with water by Monday mornings.

Sunday wasn't the only problem mine operators were having with their employees. The *Maine Mining Journal* pointed out that Maine "is the only place we ever heard of where the mining industry was compelled to come almost to a standstill during the haying season; but it is so." Workers were glad to go underground during the winter, but they expected to work their farms in warm weather.

Transporting the ore was another problem. The winter of 1880-1881 was severe, and vessels bringing supplies to the mines were frozen in ice. Often, heavy seas delayed the shipping of ore, and roads were blocked with snow.

William Morris Stewart continued to have faith in Maine's mining industry. The failures he attributed entirely to management. Silver required costly stamping mills to process cleanly, and most of the mines around the state failed because of inadequate stamping equipment. Wherever Stewart went, testimonials were given in his honor. For nearly a year he had been ill with recurrence of a fever he got while he was a soldier in Central America. On June 5, 1882, he collapsed and died at the Crawford House in Boston at the age of 54.

Frank Bartlett, who was responsible for starting the gold and silver rush in Maine, was now disenchanted and moved to Denver. He and the Governor of Colorado were close friends. Once settled in Denver, Bartlett speculated in Colorado mines and raced the first roadsters up Pike's Peak.

Stewart was spared the events that followed. Maine's heyday of copper, gold and silver mining was over. Within a week after his death, stocks fell steadily and sharply all over the country. There would be a few encouraging signs in the months ahead, but there was no recovery. Then came the recession of 1883. In the end, a million dollars invested yielded only $35,000 worth of metals. The *Maine Mining Journal* now had no news to fill its pages, and the publication would soon appear as the *Maine Mining and Industrial Journal.* In one of its last issues an explanation was offered to its dwindling subscribers.

"Mining exchanges are now reaping the reward of their numerous deals, bear raids, repudiations of contracts by members etc., etc., and unless relief soon comes from some unexpected quarter, it would seem that they cannot much longer exist."

In the first issue of the *Maine Mining and Industrial Journal,* there was an item in the personal column announcing that Colonel Darling had purchased a mineral tract in Nova Scotia. The remainder of the space in the column was devoted to woolen and pulp mills, shoe and canning factories.

The Quoddy Hoax

Shortly after taking over as pastor in a small church in De Land, Florida, the Reverend Prescott Ford Jernegan, in the late fall of 1896, wrote a letter to a former associate, Arthur B. Ryan, a successful jeweler and a Deacon of the First Baptist Church in Middletown, Connecticut.

"My Dear Deacon Ryan: A few nights ago I had a dream during which it was revealed to me that GOLD can be extracted from the ocean by passing a current of electricity through chemically treated quicksilver. The dream was so vivid, I tried the experiment in a small way, AND IT WORKS!

Now if we can get someone to finance a factory for doing this work on a big scale, we would soon be millionaires."

If this letter had come from another person, Ryan would have thought that here was someone who was insane or out to swindle him. But he knew and liked this pastor who came from one of the older and respected families on Martha's Vineyard, Massachusetts. Instead of taking over his father's whaling vessel, Jernegan studied chemistry before switching to the ministry and graduating from both Brown University and Newton Theological School. It was Ryan who had helped Jernegan get his first pastorate in Middletown, Connecticut.

Soon there had been disagreement in the deacon's house of worship. Men of the cloth were expected to preach the gospel and leave the running of the church to an elected board. Ryan was outraged when parishioners objected to Jernegan's flamboyant style of preaching. The flock liked the pastor's young wife, Evelyn, but when the Reverend Mr. Jernegan wanted to do things in his own way, such as opening a home for hobos and having them pay for their keep by splitting wood, the congregation was horrified. The board suggested a cut in salary or his resignation. Jernegan lost his temper, gave up the pastorate, and went to Florida.

Ryan, being a jeweler, knew a lot about gold, mercury and acids, and when checking his encyclopedia he remembered that in every ton of seawater there was the presence of gold, silver, and other valuable metals. He also knew that scientists had been trying to find some inexpensive way of getting gold from the sea. And here was this letter from Reverend Jernegan claiming that the method had been given to him in a dream.

The deacon had just the man to finance the factory—his close friend, Andrew N. Pierson, in nearby Cromwell, Connecticut. Pierson was the founder of what was then the world's largest network of greenhouses, and a man who was honest and decent in every way.

Ryan was certain that he could get "Andy" to see the potential of such an invention. All the pastor had to do was come North and give a successful demonstration.

What Ryan didn't know was that Jernegan had met with an old boyhood chum, a Mr. Charles Edward Fisher, student of medicine, floorwalker in a department store, and a professional deep-sea diver. C. E. was a hearty man with a flowing handlebar mustache, lover of saddle horses, women, and good wine cellars; someone who was friendly with everybody and believed the world was a place where people should be encouraged to help themselves to anything they dearly wanted. Together, Jernegan and his friend carefully planned the demonstration. It was then that C. E. was made a full partner and a confidential assistant.

Jernegan was waiting for Ryan and Pierson on the platform at the Providence, Rhode Island railroad station. It was a cold February day in 1897, and he had just come up from Florida. Jernegan hated the stiff wind that outlined a bottle-like bulge under his thin coat. He wondered if the two men would bring the things he requested. When the two stepped from the train, both wearing bulky coats and mittens, Jernegan saw that they were carrying a heavy basket, a lantern, and two small oil stoves. They had come prepared.

The three men got into the sleigh that Jernegan had rented and rode to the waterfront. There they stopped by a long wharf, lighted the lantern, and hitched the horse. At the end of the pier, high above the ocean, was a small shed. The clergyman got out a key and unlocked the door. There wasn't much inside, only a couple of broken chairs, a small table, and some storage batteries and wires. A heavy piece of sacking covered the one tiny window, and the trapdoor in the floor was bolted.

The box Jernegan had asked the two Connecticut men to carefully construct was made of wood and lined with zinc. It had a cover, and there were several holes so water could flow in and out. Into this box they emptied three vials of quicksilver and the mysterious chemical that Jernegan was carrying in a glass-stoppered bottle. The electrolytic action as the current passed over the wires in the box would attract the gold, he promised them, and the mercury and his secret solution would do the rest.

"All you have to do is attach the wires from the box to the battery, close the cover, and lower away. I'll come for you as soon as it's daylight." And with a smile, Jernegan added: "Oh yes, and don't forget to throw the switch. Well, good night, gentlemen, and good luck!" Then Jernegan walked back to the sleigh and drove to a fashionable hotel where he had registered.

All through the night, Ryan and Pierson kept watch as they shivered by the two smoky oil stoves. It was imperative that no one tamper with the box. At dawn, the frozen men were just prying open the trapdoor when Jernegan arrived. The box was quickly pulled up from the depths. If Ryan and Pierson had expected to find a handful of gold, they would have been disappointed. But an assay of the mercury shining on the zinc inside the box revealed that during the night Jernegan's contraption had collected about $4.50 worth of pure gold.

There was one unexplained and rather unsettling thing that did happen during the course of the demonstration. Some of the mercury inside had escaped. Jernegan quickly reminded the two that they had built the box themselves and had provided their own mercury and the device had been on the floor of the ocean all the time they were in the shed.

"Look at the facts, gentlemen," Jernegan smiled. "If one small box and a bit of mercury can accumulate almost $5.00 in pure gold from the ocean in a single night, just think what we could do with, say, one thousand of these little boxes!"

Ryan and Pierson already had been thinking about the possibilities. But before they would say anything to their friends about investing money for a factory, they suggested other demonstrations. It was something Jernegan was about to recommend; he wanted them to be absolutely confident in his invention before a penny was spent. Further experiments were conducted in other places along the coast: more in Rhode Island, some in Connecticut, and one very encouraging test was made on the lonely shores of Block Island. While the amounts of gold varied, there was always more than enough to convince the two that Jernegan's box was a marvelous success.

C. E. Fisher was never around when Jernegan poured the magic formula into the box to mix with the mercury, but C. E. was hard at work. Dressed in a diving suit and carrying an extra supply of compressed air, Fisher was busy salting the box with gold.

On November 5, 1897, a group of businessmen gathered at the law office of Levi Turner in Portland, Maine. They were there to form a corporation to extract gold from the ocean. With the exception of C. E. Fisher, who came as a "dear friend" of Jernegan's, these men all had been successful in business, and many of them were prominent church members.

"We'll call it the Electrolytic Marine Salts Company," Jernegan told the group, "and I think, gentlemen, we should capitalize it for ten million shares at a par value of one dollar a share."

They all agreed and papers were signed. Each director of the corporation purchased one share of stock, and the remaining 9,999,995 shares were made available to Jernegan and Fisher with the agreement that they were to hire agents to sell the stock to the public.

The Reverend Prescott F. Jernegan, who now wished his name to be printed on company stationary as Mr. P. F. Jernegan, had no difficulty in getting himself elected as Vice President and General Manager. The other officers were Arthur B. Ryan, President; C. E. Fisher, Assistant General Manager; W. R. Usher, Treasurer; and A.

P. Sawyer, Member of the Board of Directors. The last two named were respected businessmen from Massachusetts. When asked as to where the first factory should be located, Jernegan was ready with an answer.

"Brother Fisher and I have made extensive explorations, and we have found an ideal location at North Lubec, Maine, on Passamaquoddy Bay." He explained that the abnormal rise and fall of tides in the area would be perfect for the harvesting of gold. "The place is remote, and the seas saltier, and there will be less chance of inquisitive competitors poking around."

The Electrolytic Marine Salts Company soon became a sensation. Everyone wanted to put money into it. Clergymen, aware of Jernegan's background, gave their life's savings willingly, and bankers and lawyers came running with open checkbooks. Even relatives begged Jernegan to take their money to use in building his factory.

Jernegan never turned anyone down. Hiring agents to sell stock wasn't necessary after all. The financial community along the entire East Coast was impressed with his invention, but still he insisted on more demonstrations. He even got a group of scientists to study the mercury before it was immersed, and when the box came up heavy with gold, more investors were clamoring to be taken into the company.

An old gristmill at North Lubec was hurriedly converted. A board fence 10 feet high with 3 strands of barbed wire on top surrounded the complex, and a 700-foot dam with automatic gates was built to control the flow of water. Stables and cottages were erected near the plant for officials of the corporation to use when visiting, and several year-round residences in Lubec were renovated. When the noonday whistle sounded, more than 600 workers dropped what they were doing and opened their dinner pails.

Word of mouth did the rest. There were tales of large shipments of gold coming from the plant to the government assay office, and even armed guards on special trains. Silver, as well as gold was shipped from the well-concealed and fortified Plant No. 1. There were plans for Plant No. 2 to have thousands of Jernegan's boxes.

No effort was made to silence such talk; officials of the company liked the publicity. A gold brick was on display in the corporation's Boston office for the benefit of both stockholders and future investors. "We've spent $50,000 on this plant," President Ryan told a group of visitors. "The new one will cost ten times as much. At present, we have 243 machines working and each one collects about $1.27 worth of gold out of the ocean every twenty-four hours."

Klondike Plant No. 1
and Prescott Jernegan.

In order to square his gold adventure with his religion, or perhaps unable to squelch the preacher part of his complicated makeup, the Reverend Mr. Jernegan preached a sermon shortly after his arrival in Lubec, at an evensong service led by Andrew Pierson. "Let us turn our backs on the things of this earth, and look to the abode of bliss and glory," he told the gathering. But this was no time to take such heed as all of Lubec was hypnotized by his magic gold accumulators.

The Church that Jernegan Built

This preacher always made certain that poor people got their money, and he never dickered when he bought property from them along the West Lubec shore. If a poor man wanted $2,000 for land worth only a tenth of the asking price, Jernegan gladly paid the full amount. But if he thought one had funds, he was unscrupulous and quick to take advantage.

As a special treat to a group of investors, Jernegan displayed the accumulators. He lighted a lantern and took his guests down a flight of stairs where a door made of heavy planks was securely locked. This opened into a long chamber under a pier with several walkways running the entire length. There the investors saw underwater pipes that forced seawater over the gold collecting devices. These were kettle-shaped machines about 30 inches in diameter and containing measured amounts of mercury and acids.

"These accumulators," Jernegan explained, "attract gold out of the seawater at the rate of a dollar a day for each machine. We have 250 of them now. But Plant No. 2 will have 5,000." Then he described the site of the proposed factory. It was going to be perfect for their needs. "There's no end to it really. Why do people insist on going to the Klondike, I ask you? There's gold enough on every Quoddy tide to pay the National debt."

The sale of stock was going faster than Jernegan expected, and true to his belief in giving the poor a chance to benefit from a good thing, he issued from his Boston office 350,000 shares at a dollar a share. This meant a person could buy into the company for as little as a dollar, and there were a lot of poor people who were willing to invest. Within three days all the shares had been sold.

But C. E. Fisher was having difficulties keeping up with the monstrous appetite of the accumulators. Every week the company shipped a load of gold to the assay office in New York, and this meant Fisher had to scurry about buying old watches, rings, lockets and chains, anything gold to keep renewing the supply. Somehow, he was able to find just enough to salt the kettles on his nightly diving excursions in the icy waters under the pier.

The selling of stock continued, and more shipments of gold went from the plant to the assay office, but a rumor started that the payment of some bills had been delayed. To silence such talk, the company made sure that more money circulated in Lubec, and more people in town were quickly added to the plant's payroll. Then to improve his image, Jernegan built a church, preached in it, and baptized converts. But the next issue of stock was a disaster. Someone found out that the Electrolytic Marine Salts Company was spending a dollar and ten cents to get a dollar's worth of gold. To local residents and investors, this was highly suspicious and no way to do business.

Then one morning the kettles were pulled from the depths and there was no gold in the accumulators! Paymaster Frank Gillise had to lock his door when an angry crowd threatened to lynch him. Local men who were earning big wages at the plant wept openly. Jernegan mounted a barrel, and in an unsteady voice told them that the money was gone. He assured them that their wages would be paid from the sale of the machinery and lumber. Violence was somehow averted, and the crowd left, cursing and looting their way back to their homes.

At the moment that Jernegan was trying to calm the angry crowd, Charles Edward Fisher, with a heavy portmanteau under his arm, was boarding the steamer General Leavitt for New Brunswick. He was on his way to parts unknown, with the payroll and several bricks of gold, never to see his country again. It was later learned that he fled to Australia where he died penniless and unmourned by his relatives on Martha's Vineyard.

Jernegan did what he could to meet the payroll and to soothe those investors who were threatening him with prison. Then, just before he was to be taken into custody, he also disappeared from Lubec. Jernegan had already made financial preparations for such a move. Applications for loans had been placed at two New York banks for the purpose of buying platinum wire, and when the National Shawmut Bank in Boston gave a satisfactory credit rating, the requests for funds were approved. Jernegan withdrew $90,000.

Why did Fisher and Jernegan run away with small sums prematurely? They weren't under suspicion, and they could have absconded with $10,000,000 as easily as the estimated $350,000 between them. There may have been some disagreement over the percentage of the spoils. When Jernegan was caught by a reporter in Grand Central Station in New York, the unhappy businessman and former preacher tried to explain his position.

"Nothing fraudulent on my part," he assured the newsman. "But I cannot conceal from you the fact that my fellow manager, Charles Fisher, has disappeared. A very practical man, you know. I hardly know what to do without him. Especially, as he has carried off the formula. But I am tracking him, and expect to get it back."

The Pinkerton Detective Agency was hired to find Jernegan, but they never located him. On July 23, 1898, he sailed to France with his wife, son, and $100,000 in cash and bonds. But then, only a few months later, somewhere in the depths of this man on the run, decency or conscience led him to make a surprising move. He sent back $75,000 to his creditors, keeping the remaining $25,000 which he must have felt was his by good right.

Then the lust for gold caught Jernegan again while he was visiting England, and unbelievable as it seemed to those who had been cheated, he lost $30,000 in his own kind of scheme. Some British inventors were trying to extract the precious metals from seawater. Jernegan studied their efforts and was convinced that they had truly found the formula. He invested nearly all his savings and was swindled the way he had swindled others.

Jernegan later returned to the United States, and for some years worked to salvage his life. He acquired new friends, made a modest fortune dealing in small commodities in New York, and then lived for a time in Hawaii. When the people of Lubec, Maine last heard of his travels, Prescott Ford Jernegan was teaching school somewhere in the Philippines.

Other Diggings and Drillings

The seventy-five old gold mines scattered throughout Maine were limited operations. Most of them had only one or two shafts, and when these mines didn't produce, the stockholders were left holding worthless certificates. But interest has never faded. Commercial mining companies drilling for zinc and copper deposits still consider gold the frosting on the cake. Today's problem is operational costs. It is impractical to mine for gold, though some mining engineers believe that it is only a matter of time before someone stumbles upon such a mine.

More space than this book provides would be needed to tell the full story about these old mines. A few of them should be mentioned, along with the expectations and disappointments. These mines are a part of Maine's history, and they could be part of its future as well. They are still there waiting for some adventurous miner to drill deeper into an old tunnel or shaft.

One of the ledges that got blasted during the time when hundreds of pastures were being dug up was located in Guilford, Maine. Not many people living there today would think of their town as a likely place for a gold rush—yet 125 years ago on the farm of Lysander Bennett such a thing nearly happened. It was in 1864 that rocks on a ledge were found to contain not only silver and copper but gold as well.

After the formation of a company, papers were signed for mineral rights and the conditional purchase of the property. A tunnel six feet square was blasted into the hillside and toward an outcropping in a ledge. The operation was known as the Bennett Silver Mine of the Guilford Gold Mine. This dual title had something to do with the pending purchase of the land—some relatives of Lysander claimed that the officers of the company wanted him to think that silver was the only ore to be found.

Machinery in those days was slow and expensive. Though the work progressed satisfactorily enough, the company failed to find rich ore. The mine was soon abandoned.

Some local people disagreed with these findings. There was great wealth locked in the ledge, and the tunnel didn't go far enough. The officers lost courage because there had been an explosion in the mine that had killed the company's president; had they gone on something would have been found. When asked where the president had been buried, one official stated that cremation had taken place out of state. No, he wouldn't say just where—for the sake of the family and their right of privacy.

An accidental shooting at the mine site several years later sparked more controversy and superstition—the mine was jinxed. This time a Guilford man had lost his life, and people around town felt that the shaft should be closed.

But there was gossip on the lighter side. Some residents claimed that enough silver had been taken from the tunnel to make a silver tea service which had been presented to a local dignitary. Years later, when asked who this person was, a lady replied: "I know but I can't really say. There are still living relatives."

Even today, one can see from the top to the bottom of a hill, near Guilford Center, the scars of an old gold and silver mine. Rock collectors visiting the mine find it challenging. There are specimens of pyrite, copper ore, galena, zinc ore, and quartz.

Owls Head seems such an unlikely place for gold mines, but in the 1860s there were several shafts in this coastal community below Rockland. One 20-foot pit was sunk just east of Easter Cove. Another less than a mile away, known as the Berry Mine, was more than 30 feet deep. Shafts also were dug on two farms outside Owls Head, and further down the shore, south of town, a shaft of more than 70 feet was sunk in which gold and silver ores were found.

The Rockland Courier-Gazette, in its March 18, 1939 issue, carried a story telling how a Mr. John Westlund filled a 40-foot shaft with rocks, stumps, and alders, and planted a garden. The mine shaft had been dug by an unidentified Bangor man who, according to the newspaper, was a "gold fiend."

Although the Milton Mine in Sullivan stayed open only a short time and was forced to close because of a lack of paying ore, there was a point in its operation when the owners were sending encouraging reports to the *Maine Mining Journal.* An excerpt from this publication in 1880 was geared to stockholders and future investors.

"The Milton Mine's three regular working crews are daily employed on each shaft. No. 1 is now down 110 feet and in vein matter of a very favorable nature. Machinery for the mill is upon the ground and will be put up and set in operation at once. Everything about the mine betokens of prosperity. The machinery is all paid for and the outstanding indebtedness is very small."

Another Sullivan mine, the Golden Circle, located on Suet Island, tried a different way of attracting investors. They posted an announcement in several publications stating that "a three and a half ounce gold bar, the results of working 545 pounds of ore from the Golden Circle may be seen at the American Mining Bureau, No. 63 Broadway, N.Y.C."

Great hopes also were placed on the Lone Star Mine in Woodstock, Maine. In the 1880s, an assay revealed 278.6 ounces of silver per ton and 43.02 ounces of gold. Unfortunately, the yield soon was found to be disappointing and the mine was abandoned.

In recent years, some mines had encouraging assays, only to have hopes dashed by the next day's drilling. "The mining industry, producing copper, zinc, and lead, look upon gold as a by-product," explained Bill Garrett. "But the gold from these mines can sometimes be more valuable than the copper and zinc. I've been to the Black Hawk Mine over at Blue Hill and seen their processing plant. The guide showing us around didn't mention a word about gold and silver, but there must have been some reason why he didn't."

There is a gold mine on Raymond Hill, only a few miles from the village of Gray, Maine. Before the turn of the century, when roadwork was being done in the area, a lot of ore was blasted and samples were sent to Augusta to be assayed. The report showed the ore was rich in gold. But transportation was poor in those days, and it was decided it would cost too much to ship the ore by rail.

"So the project was dropped," states an old news clipping, "but there are elderly folks at Raymond Hill today who are confident there is a lot of gold there, and that some day it will make folks rich."

In 1944, Archie Gordon of East Franklin, Maine, claimed that he had discovered a gold mine in Hancock County. Gordon produced a specimen of ore the size of his fist with specks of gold running through it. His report of a vein several hundred feet in width and more than a mile long wasn't believed. Gordon, who had a reputation of being dependable and honest, wouldn't reveal where in Hancock County the mine was located. His reason for keeping the site a secret was that he didn't want the Maine scenery ruined by a gold rush.

The most publicized of recent discoveries was at the Dolsan Mine in Pembroke, Maine. Its president, Charles Robbins, surprised the mining world when he announced on August 23, 1965 that drill findings of a 9.7 foot strip showed 3.85 ounces of gold per ton. "It is the most spectacular drill hole finding on the East Coast," Robbins told reporters. In addition, the same strip revealed 3.14 ounces of silver per ton, and 2.44 percent of the ore was copper. In a wider part of the same drill hole, 2.15 ounces of gold per ton of ore were found in a 17.3 foot strip.

Robbins, an American citizen living in Montreal, with a second home near his Dolsan property, was 43 when he announced his astonishing drill finding. He had entered the mining scene from the brokerage end of the business. Robbins had been connected with exploratory mining for nearly ten years and was president of five mining companies at the time of the Pembroke drilling. One of the companies he operated was the Black Hawk Mine.

An encouraging aspect of the Pembroke discovery was that the relatively inexpensive open pit method of getting the ore out of the ground would be used. An application for a government loan to finance further exploration work had been made. In a press release from Augusta, Governor John Reed estimated that at least 10 years of mining was in the offing at Pembroke. "To the people of Maine as well as to the mining industry generally," explained Governor Reed, "the discovery of metal resources in Maine has occurred at a remarkable rate. Within four years, with state assistance there have been three major fields, the Black Hawk operation at Blue Hill, Callahan Mining at Harborside, and now the Dolsan Mines Ltd. at Pembroke."

Early in January of 1966, Dolsan Mines was reported to be the second most active stock during 1965 on the Canadian Stock Exchange with more than 32 million shares changing hands.

As the months of 1966 went by and new drill holes were made at Pembroke, much of the glitter left the operation. Copper and silver contents were reported as quite high but the gold dropped, assaying only .10 ounces per ton in the first hole and .14 in the second at a greater depth. Geologist Dave Ross of Calais, Maine, representing Dolsan, assured reporters that the firm was quite optimistic about Pembroke as a mining possibility. "Since we were primarily interested in copper," said Ross, "the drop in gold content does not discourage hopes for mining the areas."

Shortly afterwards, Robbins shifted his attention to a mercury mine in Nevada. It was a small operation, but one that could be expanded, "You can never tell what's next with Charlie Robbins," said a reporter in a Bangor newspaper.

The Keith, Glines, and Winthrop Mines

In October 1936, when the Sheriff of Androscoggin County told his men that they were going to dredge the old Keith Mine in Livermore for a missing hunter, the deputies assumed that the sheriff was talking about some quarry. So many of these open pits dented the landscape where mica and feldspar had been mined commercially. But what the men found was a shaft that dropped more than 50 feet.

Most people in Livermore today have never heard of this old gold mine, but it caused excitement around the turn of the century. If the operation had succeeded, the name of Martin L. Keith's uncle would still be remembered in the Lewiston area. In newspaper articles, he is mentioned only as "a member of the family." This uncle who married a Keith was a forty-niner who failed to find his fortune in California. But he did return to Maine with a knowledge of the types of formation likely to bear gold. The restless man roamed his brother-in-law's farm and one day came upon an interesting outcropping in a swamp. He studied the strata, took several samples and went back to the Keith farmhouse. After the uncle talked long and hard about untold riches waiting for them all, Martin Keith and his father, Marcus, began paying attention. Perhaps there was something to all this raving. But the site wasn't very promising. Who would expect to find gold in a swamp full of stagnant pools and muck pits?

The Keiths were hardworking farmers, and a gold mine was something to play with after the hay was in and the corn harvested. Young Martin Keith had yet to find his life's work. At the time of the gold discovery, he would have been the last to think that he would one day be a well-known gem cutter.

As they were discussing where to send samples, Martin remembered one of his teachers at Bowdoin College. Professor Robinson could tell if it was worthwhile. He replied immediately and suggested that the Keiths start excavating to see if the ore continued to assay well at lower levels.

The first pit, Shaft No. 1, was 10 feet square and went to a depth of 20 feet before it was abandoned. Further digging revealed a seam in the solid rock on the east side of the pit. Samples of the ore were taken by persons who were not involved in the mine and assays showed considerable increases. One ran $84, another $96, and one ran as high as $105 per ton. Scattered samples of ore were taken from Shaft No. 1, and sent to J. B. Darling at a refinery and smelting plant in Providence, Rhode Island. Darling's analysis came as no surprise to the Keiths.

"February 4, 1892. Statement: Ore presented by M. L. Keith, Auburn, Maine. Description: Quartzite with iron pyrites; gold, per ton - 2,000 lbs - 10 oz. $9.00. Total per ton $27.54. The ore seems to run quite well and would bear further proof as at the above figure it could be made to pay if worked in a large way. Respectfully, J. B. Darling."

Work on Shaft No. 2 was done at first by members of the Keith family, from 1892-1896. When they had time and money to spare, they hired a few neighbors, bought hand drills, and set off a few explosives. The Keiths had discovered the direction of the vein when they sank Shaft No. 1, but the family was seriously handicapped by lack of capital. Since the vein was now about a foot thick and assayed from $30 to $40 a ton, they had no way of knowing if it would dwindle to nothing or continue to a mother lode.

Marcus Keith was unable to come to a decision on the mine as he discussed the prospect with his son, brother-in-law, and neighbors. He reasoned that if more people were involved the individual risk would be less. How would he feel, and could he live with himself if he convinced his friends to invest heavily in the mine and it failed?

Samples of ore were taken again and sent to Darling. This time with lower but still encouraging results: "Sample No. 1 - gold and silver - $27.10, No. 2 - $23.95, and No. 3 - $26.13." But this assay didn't convince Marcus that they should keep digging. A period of inactivity followed, and there was no mention of the mine in newspapers from 1896 to 1903. Now it was Martin Keith who was anxious to carry on a more extensive operation at the mine. Marcus had had enough for the time and threw himself more completely into his farming, while his son began looking around for investors.

In February 1903, the Androscoggin Mining and Milling Company was incorporated under the laws of the state and given a charter. The company was formed with capital stock of $750,000. Shares were sold to interested persons and extensive advertising was carried around the state. The officers included John L. Cummings, Jr., President, a respected businessman of Livermore Falls;

Attorney John H. Maxwell, Treasurer—he was manager of the local power company; and Martin Keith and his father as members on the board of directors. They were all worthy men who believed in the company, and with such a distinguished board of officers, many families in the area invested their savings.

Now that the mine had capital, machinery was purchased, and four men were hired. A boiler was installed to furnish steam power for the pump which they hoped would keep the shafts free of swamp water. A large hogshead with a third of its top cut off was used for digging. The pit went down to solid rock, and log cribbing held the earth on top of the shaft in the form of a square box. A building was erected to be used as a storehouse and blacksmith shop. Also in the building was a furnace with crucibles and retorts for testing the ore.

Shaft No. 2 was sunk to a depth of 50 feet and the tunnel excavated 30 feet to the east. The gold-bearing rock increased in width at the lower levels, and Martin Keith and his men wondered if a lode of gold wasn't within reach.

But they had spent too much money, too quickly, and the company was unable to float any loans. They had received nothing through the sale of ore, and in order to make any return possible, they now realized that they had to handle ore in large quantities. This meant huge expenses for smelters and stamping mills, The other way of staying alive would be to mine the ore and ship it to a smelter. This they found impossible. Transportation at the time was by train, and a river with no bridge cut the mine from the railroad. The only thing to do, just when the signs were so encouraging, was to close the prospect and let the shaft fill up with water.

Martin Keith's niece, Marjorie Hodgkins of Auburn, remembered: "the last days of the gold mine and the tragedy of its failure." She realized the high hopes everyone had for its success. "So many people invested their last penny. It was no hoax, but neither enough money nor the technology was available to make a go of it." She claimed her uncle tried every possible way to keep the two shafts from flooding, but the project cost more than it was likely to produce. "I used to have some pieces of gold that were taken out of the mine," said Mrs. Hodgkins, "but I didn't know enough to value them, and I don't know what ever became of them."

Martin Keith

Years later, when Martin Keith was asked about this mining failure, his response was unexpected. He insisted that had such a discovery been made in one of the mining states in the West, the vein would have been worked until it either reached a lode of gold or dwindled to nothing. He said this was the difference between the New England view and the Western outlook.

Today, there is no sign of a building at the site, only two pits filled with stagnant water, and bits and pieces of metal. But what the Keith mine does prove is that there is gold at lower levels in Livermore, Maine.

Less than a year before Martin Keith found backers for his mine, the Mount Glines Gold and Silver Mining Company was incorporated and recorded at the Registry of Deeds at South Paris, Maine. The date was June 28, 1902. The original stockholders of the company were Ralph T. Parker, Arthur E. Morrison, J. Abbott Niles, Stanley Bisbee, and William McCrillis. These five Rumford men each held one share and the agreement called for an incorporation with 300,000 shares at one dollar.

Located in Milton Plantation, south of Rumford and near Mount Zircon, the mine went into operation early in 1903 with William McCrillis as the manager. The *Rumford Falls Evening Herald* carried the announcement of this newly formed company and referred to McCrillis as "an experienced miner."

At 11 o'clock in the morning, on May 12, 1903, an excursion train arrived in Rumford Falls. The passengers, some of whom had traveled all the way from New York City, were met by a long line of wagons to take them to the mine. One reporter counted more than 100 people participating in the festivities. The guests were taken into the mine and shown the various tunnels and were given small bags so they could gather samples for analysis or souvenirs.

"We are informed by Mr. McCrillis," stated the *Herald,* on May 13, "that the last assay which they have got, gives $33 per ton from the samples sent away." This much gold was an encouraging sign, the visitors were assured. "McCrillis declares that the party only saw one edge of the mine. The stock, he also announces may be bought at present at 60 cents per share, but will be advanced in price in a month."

Then the guests were led to a "delicately arrayed table on the mountain side" for a banquet of baked beans, delicious salads, a variety of cakes and gourmet coffees. "Plenty of evidence that never before were so many words of praise used about a meal."

A complete crushing and sorting plant was installed at the Glines, made possible by large amounts of money invested by out of state stockholders, particularly by businessmen from the New York and Boston areas. The elaborate equipment was to be used in separating the gold from the ore, and the five principal stockholders were so confident of success that many prominent Rumford families were caught up in a wave of gold fever.

The mining was done in a quartz dike, and the ore consisted of pyrite, pyrrhotite, and chalcopyrite. How much gold was found has never been revealed, but rumors persist even to this day that gold was loaded into a shotgun and blasted into the quartz just before the prospective stock buyers arrived for their picnic.

Dean McCrillis, grandson of the Glines manager, didn't know if any gold was found in the prospect. "I guess there was some," he went on. "Down at my office in Rumford (The Plumbago Mining Company) there is a small crucible that says 'Glines Mine.' I think my grandfather was involved in wishful thinking."

There must have been some hope of finding a productive amount of gold from the ore as a shaft of 150 feet was sunk and a tunnel of 300 feet was drilled into the mountain. The profits came from an unexpected source; a large amount of apatite was found. It proved enough to convert the operation into a phosphate mine. "They made fertilizer," said Dean McCrillis, "and that worked very well. They did have use of the mill they set up." Then, remembering a photograph of the mine, McCrillis recalled "a sluice type of rig coming off the mountain. They ground the phosphate, and they bagged it."

But mining for fertilizer wasn't enough to satisfy the investors or sustain the founders. By 1906, this mining venture was over. A news item in the May 1908 issue of the *Rumford Falls Times* announced that J. Abbott Niles had been appointed receiver for the Mount Glines Gold and Silver Mining Company. There was a petition of the trustees under the mortgage to secure an issue of $50,000 in bonds.

The promoters of the mine were quickly called swindlers by their critics, and some of the investors would have tried to jail the five original stockholders had there been no phosphate. In all fairness to these men who dreamed of gold being brought forth from Mount Glines, there was justification for the operation. The dike did resemble quartz found in California, and with such encouraging signs little effort was made to suppress their hopes.

Within a short time, the buildings at the mine were torn down, and the equipment left to rust. Adam Galuza remembers visiting the mine when he was a reckless teenager. "They had a section of thirty foot ladders that went down into the third level of the mine. I used to go down those soggy old ladders to the bottom to find drills that had been left. There were railroad tracks going into the mine, and before I knew it, water was up to my armpits. It's a wonder the ladders didn't break on me."

A youngster looking for drills at the lower levels of the mine was of no consequence to J. Abbott Niles, who held the receivership, but when a Mr. R. was suspected of taking a huge anvil weighing several hundred pounds the case was brought to court. Mr. R.'s lawyer was convincing as he presented his client's case to the jury. It was impossible for one human being to carry an anvil of such weight a mile to the road and home. This fact was brought up again and again. But as Mr. R. kept listening to his lawyer and feeling that his strength was being downgraded, the indignant defendant rose, and before the lawyer could stop him, Mr. R. shouted: "By thunder I did!" This admission assured the proud man of a stay in the county jail.

Stuart Martin recalls visiting the mine in recent years with a geology friend. They found little left, only dangerous shafts, a pulverized dump, and a countless number of bats on the walls of the mine. Martin's companion had a keen interest in the furry creatures and tenderly plucked one from the wall to better examine it—a curiosity that Stuart Martin didn't share with his friend. "They did an awful lot of digging at that mine," said Martin when describing the operation. "An awful lot of digging!"

The Glines Mine wasn't the only partnership that Dr. J. Abbott Niles and William McCrillis formed. They both believed that there was a sufficient amount of gold coming down the Main Branch of the Swift River to be mined commercially, and the two decided to build a giant sluice above Coos Canyon by a placer site.

The Long Tom of more than 1,200 feet was made of logs with a lining of timbers. (The exact year hasn't been established, but since the Glines Mine went into receivership by 1908, a year or two after the closing would be a realistic estimate.) Nearly 40 Mexican workmen, who had been employed by McCrillis and Niles at the Glines, were paid to shovel material into the sluice. The Mexicans camped that summer on Dingle Hill, which may account for a piece of gold that George Mattor found in the crop of a duck—Mattor built his house near the place where the Mexicans had tented.

Stories tell of the hired help sneaking to the river at night and raiding the riffles of the Long Tom for choice pieces of gold. Another rumor, which becomes more difficult to believe with the passing years, is that someone raided the Long Tom the night before McCrillis and Niles were going to clean the sluice for the entire summer's operation. $50,000 in gold is one of the estimates of the heist.

"I remember seeing some of the logs of the old Long Tom," said Kenneth Knapp. "It was just above Joe White's at Coos Canyon. They dug a ditch and somehow bypassed the river. That ditch was still there when I was a boy going to school."

The sluicing project was as much a failure as the finding of gold ore in the Glines Mine. McCrillis and Niles didn't continue the experiment longer than one summer. After a number of years, the spring floods washed away all traces of the Long Tom. Bill Garrett felt that the sluice could have been profitable had there been some way of guarding the accumulation. "You know as well as I do," said Garrett, "when someone sees a piece of gold, that person is going to be tempted to pick it up."

Twenty years after the Glines Mine went into receivership, plans for another mine were being made in another Maine town. An article in the *Lewiston Journal,* on October 5, 1928, stated that gold operations would commence the following spring on Mount Monadnock in Winthrop. A flotation type of mill was planned for the separation of gold and molybdenite.

This announcement was made by the owner of the mine after a

fourteen week study by W. N. Welton of Arizona. Welton was a mining engineer with more than forty years experience, and he came with a reputation of involvement with some of the most important mining ventures in the country.

"We've got something there!" Welton told the Lewiston reporter. "The formation of Monadnock is identical with that at the Hollinger Mine." Then Welton reminded his interviewer that the Hollinger was the greatest gold mine in Canada. The same geologic conditions applied to the Hempstead Mine too, the only difference being that "this formation at Winthrop occurred more than 400 million years ago; that at Hempstead much later."

What interested the noted engineer more than similarities was the geology of Monadnock. It was entirely different from that of the surrounding countryside—as if one of the more famous gold mines had been transported to an area where little gold had ever been found.

Welton said that a tunnel of 200 feet had been driven into the mountain, and gold assaying $7.20 to the ton of ore had been found throughout. The mining expert explained that this was in such quantity that the mine could operate at a profit. He intimated that the flotation mill would be only a temporary measure, as a study was to be conducted later on a more economical extraction of the gold.

"I guess they found a few flakes there," said Jordan Mangin, a Winthrop resident. "But no one in town ever got too excited about it." And did Mangin recall if the mine was first some mica or feldspar site? "Neither one, to my knowledge. All I know is people used to talk about an old fellow—I've forgotten his name—but he used to dig up there a lot."

The name was Briggs. Emerson Briggs of Winthrop. He knew there was gold on Monadnock, and what he took from the mine he kept to himself. For years, Briggs shoveled and picked his way into the hillside. During his lifetime, two shafts were sunk. Some of the Winthrop people who saw Briggs on his way to the mine, even during the coldest days in January, thought the old man an eccentric who didn't have enough to do to keep himself occupied; others thought him crazy. But Emerson Briggs, who had no known source of income, always appeared to have plenty of money.

A boy was keeping an eye on the old man and was determined one day to find a mother lode of gold for himself. The youngster, Charles H. Towle, became friendly with the elderly miner, and Briggs shared his knowledge of mining.

But success as an apple grower and buyer had to come first for Towle, and years went by before he obtained rights to mine Monadnock and bring engineers from Colorado to study conditions. The experts all agreed that there was gold in the mountain, though not one of them was willing to estimate how much. It was then that Towle engaged the services of the best mining engineer available, and W. N. Welton made the long trip from Arizona to Winthrop. Such studies were costly, but Towle was determined to spend whatever was necessary to unlock the fortress of quartz buried deep in the hillside.

"The ore body of the vein," said Welton, "will go down at least 1,000 feet; no one can tell how much deeper." And when asked how far the vein extended, the engineer was still cautious. "It is equally impossible to tell how far out under the lake the ore vein extends."

The lake was Maranacook. "It may be half a mile, it may be a mile and it may be a great deal further."

Why was the Winthrop tunnel never extended beyond its 200 feet? One news item suggested that the survey was too uncertain for the great expense that would be involved in enlarging the shaft. Another, and perhaps more reasonable explanation, was the Depression. This was no time to capture outside investors, and like others in the Winthrop area, Towle may have lacked the necessary funds to begin such an enterprise.

More than sixty years have come and gone since Charles Towle delayed his dream of finding riches on Monadnock. Winthrop is now a bedroom community for Augusta, and most people, many living within calling distance of the old shaft, have never heard of the mine. "A gold mine right here!" said the young woman who was checking out books at the library. "What will they think of next!"

Winthrop's former police chief, H. "Bud" Quinn, knew about Monadnock. He did his thesis on the gold mine when attending the University of Maine at Augusta. Quinn got permission from the landowner to go into the old shaft, but he may not have been the first to enter the mine after it was abandoned. The landowner's son claimed to have gone into it and found a piece of quartz laced with wires of gold. Since the young man was unable, or didn't choose to come up with the specimen, nobody in town believed him.

"I probably got permission to go in because I was the police chief at the time," explained Quinn. "There were a lot of bats in there but they weren't moving because it was in the springtime." He took a sample of quartz to show Ron Kley, his professor, who was also an assistant to the curator at the state museum. The specimen proved to be of interest to his teacher, but Quinn didn't think the quartz had traces of gold.

"Someone should pan the stream that runs at the bottom from where that old mine is located," said Bud Quinn. "There may be gold there."

Coastal Surprises

Seven-year-old Brendon Thurston was playing on a beach, somewhere near his Tremont, Maine home on Mount Desert Island, when a shiny round stone caught his attention. It looked different, and reaching down to pick it up he was surprised at its abnormal weight. It was heavier than any of the other rocks he had thrown into the surf that day. This was something to take home. Like so many collectibles, the stone was put aside and soon forgotten. There it remained in the Thurston household all the years that Brendon was growing up.

Sixteen years after that day on the beach, in early May of 1939, the boy's father, Herbert Thurston, decided to have a housecleaning. Brendon was now married with children and no longer at home. Scattered about the house were broken chairs, discarded mattresses, and a variety of odds and ends that Herbert had been threatening to burn for years. He carried the junk outside and placed it in a huge pile. On one of his trips back to the house, at the bottom of a closet, he came upon the stone.

Herbert Thurston had never examined what his son had brought home. He merely took it for what it appeared to be—a rock of unusual color. Now that he held it in his hand, he was astonished by its weight. Then he noticed a startling fact as he shifted the object from his right hand to his left. Clinging to the fingers of his right hand were yellow particles of dust. He had read about gold but had never seen any in its natural form. The only gold he knew came in the form of wedding rings and old pocket watches. Herbert got out his set of scales and found that the stone weighed seven pounds.

Not wishing to raise false hopes and to get his son excited over nothing, Thurston carefully wrapped the object and mailed it to a firm that he thought could identify it. If it had value, his son certainly could use the money. Brendon had to depend on WPA earnings for a livelihood. Herbert Thurston didn't have long to wait; within a few days, the answer came. The stone that had been kicking around the house for all those years was mostly gold.

Both father and son kept the discovery to themselves, but the news soon leaked from the firm where the stone had been analyzed. Several newspapers in Maine carried the story. One banner headline, on May 23, 1939, surprised many Mount Desert residents: CHILD'S CURIOSITY BRINGS RICHES TO TREMONT FAMILY.

The piece of gold weighed about seven pounds, but compressed throughout were other substances. A New York firm assayed it, and this time the report was kept confidential. Rumors had placed the estimate as high as five pounds of gold. Even at $32 an ounce, this was a fortune for a young man who was earning only a few dollars a week.

Brendon Thurston never revealed the exact spot where the nugget was found, and there was talk on Mount Desert that he had forgotten just where on the island he had been that day. No doubt, he went back to see if there were more of them on the beaches.

But young Thurston didn't keep everything to himself when talking to reporters. He told them that tucked away somewhere in a tin can was a handful of gold dust that he had rubbed off the nugget many years back. He thought the can was in the attic, and he predicted that it would take him at least three days to find it.

More interesting than the composition of this lump of gold or Brendon Thurston's can of gold dust is how a seven pound object containing five pounds of gold got on a beach at Mount Desert Island: a place where little color had ever been found. Did it come from a galleon shipwrecked off the coast, or was it unearthed by some unusual tide? And if it did come from some drift, how far from its source did it have to travel before a boy of seven picked it up?

People are surprised when nuggets are found along the coast, but it does happen. One discovery occurred even before the official 1854 first strike in Madrid, Maine. As with the Thurston nugget, there was no geologic explanation.

Henry Merryland of Harpswell Center was becoming dissatisfied with the size of the clams he was digging on a flat near his home. He wanted bigger ones to use as trawl bait. Deciding to look elsewhere, he rowed over to the Gosling Islets in Casco Bay. The year was 1850, and the gold rush in California was the chief topic of conversation in town.

The digging was better than he had hoped, and Henry decided to fill a barrel—all that his small boat could carry without sinking.

In the middle of his labors, Henry turned up a huge chunk of clay. There, amid a tangle of clams, was a gold nugget larger than his thumbnail. He had heard enough stories about gold in recent months to identify it. Not being a person easily sidetracked, Merryland pocketed the find and continued digging until the barrel was full.

When he returned to the mainland, he told no one but his wife what had happened. The next day, and the day after, he returned but was rewarded only with clams. Then Henry made the mistake that gold hunters often make when a nugget is found—he talked about it.

Soon the Goslings were lined with men digging frantically along the flats. No more nuggets were unearthed, though one digger turned up a few flakes near the place where Henry came across the clay.

Merryland never talked about his find again, and gold was a subject that no longer interested him. When asked to show off the nugget, he would shake his head. It had been misplaced. Only once did he mention the Goslings. "I don't go out there anymore," he told a fisherman. "I get my clams closer home."

There was also the Cape Jellison find by Joe Larabee of Winterport, Maine. Larabee had chased the mother lode on both sides of the United States, and one of his dreams was to work a mining claim in Alaska.

No one was more surprised than Joe when he and his brother, Allen, and two friends, Charles and Stephen Reynolds, found a specimen of gold in a ledge on the Squaw Point side of Cape Jellison, north of Belfast in Penobscot Bay. Henry Buxton, who wrote a column for the *Bangor Daily News,* interviewed Stephen Reynolds one July day in 1936 shortly after the discovery.

"At least Joe Larabee, the man with mining experience, declared that it was gold of a very rich quality," wrote Buxton. The four men had been clearing alders and digging a trench to drain a patch of ground for a property owner. "The pick of Allen Larabee peeled off a big slab from a ledge, and Joe Larabee picked up a piece of the rock, and after a minute examination let out such a strenuous whoop that five scraggly crows nearly fell out of the top of a nearby pine." As the crows flew away, the three men crowded around Joe. "Gold!" he shouted. "By godfrey boys, it's gold!" The three stared at the slab of rock, and then they all joined in and did a war dance around their find.

At first, Stephen Reynolds was reluctant to talk about the incident, but after some coaxing he brought out a rock which, according to the journalist, was "thickly veined with some kind of a glistening yellow metal." Buxton, who admitted being "no geologist," was unable to say "whether it was gold or tin or anything else for that matter."

Reynolds told Buxton that specimens of the rock had been sent to an assayer in Bangor. They were expecting a report soon. "But Joe Larabee says it's gold," said Reynolds, "and he should know as he has had a lot of mining experience in the West."

The end of the adventure came sooner than the four expected, and like most gold discoveries in Maine, the conclusion was a disappointing one. The assay was all that Joe Larabee expected. The rock they chipped from the ledge did contain gold and of a high content. But what Larabee didn't know, and no miner can ever predict, was how much gold remained. In the case of the Cape Jellison find, nothing else was found in the ledge or around Squaw Point. They had it all when they started their war dance.

A more recent coastal surprise occurred in Ogunquit in 1960. The town needed a new parking lot, and a ton of gravel was dredged from the Josias River and dumped in nearby Perkins Cove. An Army Corps of Engineers officer saw what he thought were flakes of gold in the gravel. He got a pan, and on his first try he found a small gold nugget and a half thimbleful of flakes. That was on Thursday.

Early Saturday morning, more than 2,500 gold hunters from six states rushed the gravel heap. Some even came with cake pans, clam hoes, and frying pans. Before noontime, the place was in an uproar, and Police Chief Chris Larsen declared that he was buying a burro and staking a claim for himself. "I'm keeping everybody out of here," he shouted at reporters. "You people go away!"

The Town of Ogunquit had hired the Corps of Engineers to do the dredging, and an army spokesman suggested that the gravel had washed down from Mt. Agamenticus in York ages before. Nervous town officials had the engineers plow the gravel under, and before it could be dug up again, the parking lot was paved.

Dowsing with Lambert and Longley

The practice of dowsing to locate water has been going on for as long as people can remember in Maine, but the state has had few dowsers of gold. There are as many believers as there are skeptics when someone cuts a witch hazel stick or bends a coat hanger to search for water. Dowsing for metals and minerals draws more negative reactions. Most onlookers smile and shake their heads when someone turns to a divining rod to pinpoint gold on a river or tourmaline in a mass of cleavelandite. Maine did have its Henry Gross, a person with extraordinary dowsing ability, as described by Kenneth Roberts, but today, most dowsers in the state spend their time tracking water.

Richard Longley and Daniel Lambert were the two dowsers to get the most attention on the Maine gold scene. Longley was featured in several newspaper articles, and he appeared to have definite dowsing skills; Lambert grabbed headlines because he had a knack for swindling.

A few years before the forty-niners were rushing overland in wagons to California, Daniel Lambert was claiming that he had found vast quantities of buried treasure in Maine through the use of witch hazel sticks. He produced hundreds of pieces of battered brass as proof of his ability to locate valuable metals in the ground, and so convincing was his forthright way of explaining his skills, it wasn't long before people from all over the state were out dowsing and digging.

Lambert's favorite spot was in the hills around Pittston. He was frequently seen holding his dowser while his body convulsed with strange vibrations. Then one day the entire Kennebec Valley was electrified when the news spread that Lambert had found gold.

Daniel Lambert didn't want anyone to think that he was a greedy man. He hoped everyone would share in his big strike. A huge shipment of gold already had been sent to Philadelphia to be minted and a general distribution of his wealth would be made available to the public. Those who were interested in becoming shareholders could invest early, and the date of the circulation of the gold coins would be September 1. Many people around Augusta, and even in towns as far north as Bingham and south as York, were eager to realize profit. Some sold their homes and farms and turned the money over to Lambert.

Finally, September 1 arrived, and Lambert was not to be found. He was never seen again holding his witch hazel stick by the empty shafts and pits in the hills around Pittston. A decade went by before it was rumored that Lambert had lived for a time above Bangor and then moved away.

Lambert Day was observed for a number of years—until the Civil War began—by those who hadn't invested in the gold coins; a cruel celebration for people who had placed their faith and life's savings in Daniel Lambert's ability to dowse for gold.

Richard Longley was considered by his Caribou, Maine neighbors to be "an honest and decent man in every way," and they believed him when he claimed that he had located five deposits of gold in Aroostook County. This was in the 1930s when hundreds of men were supporting their families by panning and sluicing the streams throughout the state. This retired woodsman and grocer didn't rely on the usual tools of a prospector. When Longley went out gold hunting, he took along his homemade dowser. Spades, crowbars, and gold pans came later. Find the gold first, then use the equipment—this was the only way he ever prospected.

Longley became interested in dowsing for gold and silver in 1895 when he was a logging boss in St. Leonard, New Brunswick. A divining rod he saw in a local store caught his eye, but when he was told it would cost him $150, he decided he would make his own.

Two bands of steel one foot long were joined to form a V, and where the two bands came together, a piece of black leather was tied to serve as a strap for the cover of a small bottle. All Longley had to do was place a sample of whatever mineral or metal he wanted for his reading into the bottle and screw on the cover. It was a simple device that could be carried in his pocket. He saw no need for a longer and more elaborate rod, and he had full confidence in his dowsing ability.

His claim of locating two deposits of gold in New Brunswick and five in northern Aroostook County was scoffed at by some people around Caribou who didn't know him well. They had heard stories of gold found in the Aroostook River, but they doubted Longley's method.

Phil Pendell, a reporter, accompanied him one November day in 1939 to the location where Longley claimed he had found ore containing gold. How much of a strike it would be, he was unable to say, but samples had been sent to Washington, D.C. The mine site was on the bank of Madawaska Stream. Longley had, with the help of several friends, dug a 40 foot trench, some 13 feet deep and 4 feet wide. An embankment kept the stream from flooding the trench entirely, but a recent rain had swamped the deepest part of the excavation.

"Still holding the rod," wrote Pendell, "he paced eastward away from the stream, and the end of the device continued to point eastward. With this as his proof, Longley said that the gold vein—about a foot and a half wide—winds along under the surface of the meadow for a half mile or more. The land, incidentally, belongs to Charles Chaloult of Caribou."

One gets the feeling, when reading the newspaper clippings, that a story abruptly ends just when it starts to get interesting. Longley refused to make public the report from the assayer's office, and reactions in Caribou were evenly divided. Some said that the mine was worthless; others swore that Madawaska Stream was another Sutter's Mill. Those who didn't believe the retired woodsman and grocer were quick to ask the one question that made Longley's claim of being able to locate gold debatable: "If a man finds so much gold, why ain't he rich?"

The Perils of a Dredger

Stella and I enjoyed panning so much that we delayed getting our first gold dredge. We weren't in any hurry to change our gold-hunting habits after finding sizeable nuggets below Carl's. Then one day—I think it was during our fourth summer of prospecting—we watched two men using a four-inch dredge on the Main Branch of the Swift River, and we knew that we were ready to begin this kind of mining.

After studying the catalogs, I decided weight was the most important consideration; we needed a machine light enough to carry. The four- and six-inch dredges were just too heavy for us to maneuver comfortably without some sort of conveyance—bigger ones would come later. We finally settled on a 65 pound, 2 1/2 -inch dredge from Keene Engineering in California. It was late fall by the time the equipment arrived, and the streams now were too cold for wading and working a suction nozzle. But I did assemble the dredge just for the pleasure of looking at it.

Since we were the owners of a machine, it was time to buy wet suits too. I had seen a lot of weekend dredgers working in waders, and they had appeared severely hampered. Diving gear gives one the capability of getting at the bottom of a stream with more maneuverability. Working in waders is hard on the back, especially when using the nozzle in knee-high water.

I shall never forget that feeling of panic when I first got into a wet suit. If one suffers from claustrophobia, it is advisable to prepare for those frightening moments when the zipper is pulled and one is locked in. Stella and I felt the same way; as if we were about to go for a walk in a space suit on a planet where the gravity was ten times that of earth.

Not everyone takes to a wet suit. I've seen so many gold hunters in Maine wearing them once or twice and then going back to waders. One mining friend, who was having health problems at the time, worked for several weeks in the icy waters up to his waist with only a pair of light summer trousers for protection. He complained of feeling too constricted in his wet suit. Another gold hunter on the Swift got into his at camp and walked more than a mile downriver where he kept his dredge. Why he didn't change at the site still mystifies me. He must have been horribly chafed before he got home that night! I don't think he ever wore his wet suit again, and he dredges every weekend all summer.

Our first dredging adventure was on the Swift by the old railroad bridge where the East meets the Main Branch. It was the first day of May, and there was snow in the mountains. We were rushing the season, and we knew it. Our problem was that we had stared wistfully at the new equipment too long not to try it out.

That first plunge into the water with a wet suit nearly took my breath away. After several moments, I found the temperature of the water tolerable, but it was hard to keep our faces from freezing as we worked without masks and snorkels. We dredged about four hours and found only a few flakes. Surprisingly, we were back the next weekend, but it was the only time we started the season that early in the year. We now wait until the third week of May before getting into the water.

We made the mistake that most dredgers make in the beginning. Instead of looking upon our equipment as something to use when the situation called for that kind of capability, we allowed our machinery to become a toy—something we could play with on weekends. It didn't matter where we dredged, just as long as we could get that suction nozzle into the water and start the engine. Gone were the days of taking samples, studying rivers, and looking for ledges and clay. Dredging for the sake of dredging went on all summer, and before we realized what was happening to us, the leaves were in flame and another gold season was over.

As usual, the winter seemed endless to me, and I had plenty of time to sit and think about all the wrong decisions we had made that year. The biggest mistake was going to the nearest and easiest place just to get our dredge into the water. Stella and I couldn't carry all our gear on our backs and walk several miles along the rivers. What we needed was a vehicle that would get us into places we had in mind. Then we heard that someone had a deer cart for sale, and we bought it.

Thus began a series of bizarre episodes as we tried to convert the cart into a vehicle for our dredging equipment. We went to a small-engine man and asked him if he could create a sort of motorized stretcher. Instead of one wheel, the cart would need two for better balance and the engine would have to be powerful enough to get our dredge up hills.

He came up with a sprocket contraption which had a bicycle chain and a throttle attached to one of the handles. We tried it out in his dooryard, and no one was happy with it.

Back to the drawing board went our dream machine, and after a lot of welding, conversations, and delays, our man produced a nightmare in which a rubberized spool with cleats rubbed against one of the bicycle tires and shoved the cart forward and backward with sudden jolts and jumps. We were all unhappy with this one. Then to the cluttered shop went the deer cart to rest until the next brain wave.

By now I had spent more money than I should have, and my patience was gone. My machine man called me one day with a new invention. This time he would give me greater power and traction; two chains would be used on a bigger engine, but unfortunately there would be no reverse, only "full chains ahead." My response was immediate. We would provide our own horsepower. "Just give me another set of handles," I told him, "and I'll pretend this whole business never happened."

It doesn't take much removal of sand and gravel from under a rounded boulder for a dredger to get into serious trouble, because rocks behave differently in water than on land. One must never forget that a boulder in the river has less gravitational stability. On a previous dredging excursion we learned this important lesson. Stella was working the nozzle between boulders, and suddenly I thought I saw one of them shift.

"Did you see that move?" I asked a dredger who had stopped for a chat.

"A boulder that big ain't going anywhere," he told me,

The man had been on the river longer than we had, and I believed him.

Stella continued working the hose underwater, and she now had her head between the two massive formations of rock.

I saw motion again and quickly stopped the engine. Stella rose when she realized there was no more suction in the nozzle. Luckily she stepped back. Without warning, the boulder that had lost its foundation of overburden slammed against the other.

"Lady," I told her, now genuinely scared, "you could have had the flattest head in both Franklin and Oxford counties. We must never take chances like that again!"

I have walked several miles through the woods to a ledge in blackfly season just to test a new crevicing tool, and when we got our second dredge I was in a rush to try that out. The gleaming three-inch machine with its five horsepower engine, five-inch underwater tube, compressor, oxygen tank, hoses, and complete hookah system led me to believe that we now had total capability for any mountain stream in Maine.

"Where do you think we should take it?" Stella asked one evening in the middle of the week.

"I suppose we should head for the place where we have found the bigger nuggets."

"You don't mean by Carl Shilling's old place?"

"Why not?"

"We can't possibly carry all that down there."

I saw her glance at the shiny pile of equipment at the far end of the porch.

"Not all at once," I replied. "We'll get it down there in three trips on the deer cart."

Stella should have resisted more strenuously. Being a treasure hunter and eager to use the new dredge, she allowed herself to be carried away with the plan.

On Friday night we loaded the pickup with our dredge, deer cart, tent, food, sundries, and a variety of shovels and crevicing tools. The truck was definitely overloaded when I closed the tailgate.

The next morning, two hours before dawn, we drove from Mt. Vernon to Byron, over the back road by Tumbledown. The first hints of daylight could be seen as we went down Bateman's Lane to the landing. It was mid-September, and there was a chill in the air as we strapped some of our gear to the cart for the first trip down the trail along the East Branch.

We crossed the stream, nearly tipping the cart over on a rock, and we took breaks every few minutes along the way. All went reasonably well until we had to get the cart over a brook. One tire sank in some sand as Stella stumbled and the load came loose. I was several minutes strapping it all back on, and by the time we had reached Carl's, where we were going to make camp, I was surprised to see that the trip down had taken more than an hour.

The old military axiom of "getting there the fastest with the mostest" wasn't working for us that Saturday. It was past noon before we had all our things in place and the tent set up. After a hurried sandwich, we launched the dredge, got into our wet suits, and started the engine.

It was nearly dark when we parked the dredge on the bank and went back to camp for a well-deserved highball, then steak on the Coleman stove. As we tossed in our sleeping bags on the hard ground, the sound of coyotes on the hillside kept waking us up as the night grew colder.

At dawn, we were shivering in thick sweaters as we cooked our bacon and eggs and sipped coffee. The ground was white with frost, and we could see our breath. While we were finishing breakfast, I glanced at the wet suits hung on a line between trees. One of the suits caught my eye; it looked as if someone were already filling it.

Thawing a frozen wet suit with warm water, and getting into it when the ground is covered with frost, is the business of foolhardy folks. We shivered our way into the river, lowered the dredge and ourselves into the current and fired the engine at full throttle. We worked the overburden to bedrock and ran a whole tank of gas before the water became noticeably warmer. By two o'clock, the engine sputtered and ran its last drop of gas. Then we cleaned the sluice and panned the concentrates.

Stella got a few flakes, and I found nothing. I did see two traces of color in my pan, but I was too disgusted with my poor showing; too disgruntled to take the time to bottle them. Better nothing, I said to myself, than saving two miserable specks!

It was getting late. We had to take our equipment back up the trail. Sunday would be over by the time we got it all out. The thought of covering that shiny new gear with a piece of canvas and leaving it all week unattended was unthinkable.

It was nearly dark when I closed the tailgate and eased my aching body into the cab beside Stella for the long drive home. I knew this was my low point as a gold dredger, and yet it was a beginning. I had a feeling that no matter what happened to me on the river in the future, I would never allow myself to be defeated quite this way again.

An Interview with Bill Garrett

William Garrett shared his knowledge of mining with hundreds of people who never dreamed that there was gold in Maine or that they would capture it themselves. People of all ages were fascinated with his instructions and stories. Not a day went by during the summer months from 1980 through 1985 that there weren't several looking for him. They would drive up Route 17, turn right at Coos Canyon in Byron, go over Dingle Hill, bear right at the tree farm, and a few hundred feet on the left would be Bill's trailer and sign which read: "Garrett's Natural Gold." Here they could buy pans, vials, magnets and jewelry. If Garrett wasn't at his trailer, he could be found either up the road at his favorite spot on the East

Branch or down on the Main Branch teaching gold panning as an instructor for the University of Maine, Augusta. Bill's last summer in Byron was in 1985. He died in December 1986.

Bill Garrett

Garrett was born and raised in Virginia, attended local schools, and joined the United States Navy during World War II. Except for a short service break in 1946-47, Garrett stayed in the navy until he retired in 1965 as a chief electrician's mate. After leaving the navy, he worked for fifteen years as a self-employed electrician, and for a short time he was employed by the Department of Fish and Wildlife. Then came gold and the river.

Bill's curiosity with his surroundings was one of the things that set him apart. He would pause in a conversation in order to identify a bird's call or to show one a plant. His interests were many. They included photography, coins, old jars and bottles, rocks, gems, wildlife, and wildflowers.

"I feel I'm the richest man in the state of Maine," Garrett once said. And perhaps it was worth a few million dollars to love the things he did. If you were one of the many who went to Byron to watch Bill Garrett check his gold pan and sluice for a flake or two, chances are you came away convinced that Bill was right in feeling the way he did about his life. I know he convinced me that he had this special wealth one winter day in 1984 when I taped this interview.

Q: When did you first pan for gold?

Garrett: Back in Virginia, when I was a teenager, my father had shown me how to pan. But I panned and panned and all I got was black sand.

Q: How did you happen to look for gold on the Swift River?

Garrett: I was reading a book about various mineral locations. The description of the Swift River sounded good to me, and I decided to give it a try.

Q: Did you have any luck in the beginning?

Garrett: I didn't get any color the first two trips. I wasn't doing it wrong like some people who come with pie tins and shovel some gravel from the bank and go home, saying: "There's no gold on this river." I just wasn't digging in the right place. Actually, Charlie Damery took me under his wing.

Q: Ah! Charlie Damery!

Garrett: Yes. I met him in 1969. Charlie had already been on the Swift for about ten years. He had a sluice box and we went together to a location he knew and I spent a full day sluicing under his instructions. I found my first piece of gold below the bridge that crosses the East Branch.

Q: How did you feel when you saw that first piece of gold?

Garrett: It's indescribable! It just gives you a thrill if you find a piece of natural gold yourself. I was bitten by the goldbug that very moment. Finding your first piece of gold is like seeing the first flowers of spring. It's a new life, a new beginning.

Q: One of the loveliest of flowers.

Garrett: It's an inorganic flower.

Q: Did you return to the Swift River frequently?

Garrett: Yes. But in 1969 I was working for the Fish and Wildlife, and I only had two days off. I would go to the Swift, stay overnight, and go back the following day. But when I completed my work with them, I planned a week at a time. Then two weeks, and some summers I would spend four weeks. 1980 was the first year I spent the entire summer on the river.

Q: That would be from May to September?

Garrett: Yes. In 1979 I went to Alaska, and when I got back I rented a camp on the Swift for one month.

Q. You were gold mining in Alaska?

Garrett: Oh yes. I panned approximately fifty different streams up there. One of them was a commercial operation located fifty miles south of Anchorage. It cost four dollars a day to pan there. I've seen quite a bit of the world, but there is no place that compares to Alaska.

Q: One of the better known miners on the Swift River was Carl Shilling. Did you ever meet him?

Garrett: I only came in contact with him four times, and I never spoke more than six or ten words to him. He was referred to by many people as "the old hermit."

Q: One hears of the jars of gold he accumulated. Do you think these reports were highly exaggerated?

Garrett: Just like a fish story. Fish get longer and longer, and gold gets bigger and bigger.

Q: How did you start teaching people to pan for gold?

Garrett: Someone would come along and say: "Do you mind if I watch?" And I'd say: "Of course not." So I'd show them how to do it. And some people I taught suggested that I shouldn't be doing this for free. This started me thinking. 1980 was the first year I charged, and if I remember correctly, I had around forty students that year.

Q: Is there a particular technique one should follow when using a gold pan?

Garrett: If you pick out a hundred gold panners, you may find one hundred techniques. There will be variations. You should get the basics and develop the things that suit you. Gold panners are individuals, and they have their own little quirks.

Q: Charging a fee for panning instructions led to other commercial activities?

Garrett: That's correct. The people I instructed wanted to know where they could buy gold pans and vials to put their gold in, and I had to send them miles away to the nearest mineral shop. So I went and got myself a state tax number, and I've been selling supplies ever since.

Q: Do you think there is a mother lode of gold in Maine?

Garrett: This is a personal opinion. But I have discussed it with geologists, and most of them agree that there is no mother lode. There could have been a few hundred million years ago when the mountains were taller—before they were worn down by glaciers and other erosions.

Q: Then you believe the gold is widely scattered?

Garrett: I've gone back into the woods and dug through the topsoil to what looked like an old river bed and panned it and found colors of gold. This is away from the stream, a hundred yards or so.

Q: Is there more gold in western Maine than in eastern Maine?

Garrett: It's pretty well known that the gold producing area runs northeast to southeast, along the range of mountains that are just about parallel with the border between Maine and Canada.

Q: Have you found platinum in Maine?

Garrett: I can't say that I have. I have found gold that was coated with mercury and it fooled me at first.

Q: How did the mercury get there?

Garrett: I've been told that back in the thirties some of the greenhorn miners put mercury into their sluice boxes. They thought the mercury would capture the small particles of gold. It probably captured some of it, but they lost the mercury into the stream.

Q: Do you operate any other equipment besides a sluice and gold pan?

Garrett: Yes. A recreational suction dredge. This is a machine which creates a vacuum at the nozzle so it will pick up sand and gravel with the water flow.

Q: What do you do with the gold you find?

Garrett: I place my gold in little holders. Two lenses, one being concave or convex, depending on the angle you are looking, and another lens flat. I fill the cavity between the lenses with small particles of gold, and a band goes around the lenses to hold them together. They can be used as pendants or earrings.

Q: Do you show these frequently?

Garrett: Yes. And everyone raves about them. Most people think that you melt gold down. If you melt it, it's just like gold from any other place in the world. But if you keep it in its natural state, it's natural Maine gold, which is unique.

Q: Do you look for other things while prospecting on the river?

Garrett: I look at everything. In 1981 I found a waterworn topaz. A colorless crystal that weighed approximately 150 karats. That topaz now belongs to the Maine State Museum.

Q: I suppose a lot of people think they are going to get rich when they go out with a gold pan.

Garrett: I've learned how to make a small income from my activities. Otherwise, it wouldn't be a way of life. I have learned the area, and I have something I figure is worthwhile to pass on to other people. What I do is really not the pursuit of happiness but the happiness of pursuit.

Q: Are there many active prospectors in the state of Maine?

Garrett: I would estimate there are eight or ten who are professionals. I only consider myself an amateur because I would need advice on where to go and what the next step should be if I ran across a commercial type of deposit. I have pursued this activity all these years from a pleasure point of view, and the only reason I charge fees and sell equipment and make jewelry is because of monetary necessity.

Q: There must be something particularly appealing to you about a river?

Garrett: Yes. I have discovered that there is a lot better rock music than the kind you get over the radio, on TV, and on recordings. When water trickles over the rocks it makes a rock music that is incomparable to any other music.

Q: And you find it on the river?

Garrett: Yes. That's where you find it. On the river.

Sandy River, Oberton and Perham Streams

In his *Mines of Maine,* Frank Bartlett outlined a prospecting trip through Franklin and Somerset counties. The excursion would take several weeks to complete if done thoroughly, and it most likely would result in some worthwhile discoveries along the way.

"I should advise following the Sandy River from Farmington to its source in Green Dale to the foot of Rangeley Lakes," wrote Bartlett. "A careful examination of the sand and the bedrock should be conducted at all available points, until the head waters are reached. Then proceeding northward, the small streams running into the lake from the east should be examined, also all the ledges in that vicinity. From there an exploration should be extended along the southern slopes of the mountains in a north-westerly direction to the head waters of the Kennebec; thence proceeding down the Kennebec examining all the tributaries as far down as Moscow. Such a line of explorations, carefully conducted by an expert prospector, would probably result in the finding of deposits of value."

Gold has been widely distributed along the Sandy River and its watershed tributaries. It is too abundant and scattered to be entirely of Canadian origin. The gold in this region is not confined to talcose schist, but can also be found in the azoic rocks.

From Sandy River Plantation to Phillips, in crevices and ledges, prospectors have been finding gold for more than a hundred years. Between Strong and Farmington, because the river is slow moving and much overburden would have to be removed to reach bedrock, little gold mining has been done. Below New Sharon, color can be dug from crevices, and only a few years ago gold was reported near Norridgewock.

The gold in the Sandy River is free gold, and some prospectors believe there is a rich lode somewhere in the mountains at the headwaters. Gold hunters have explored the area, but efforts to locate the source have failed. A study of crevices along the Sandy

—in places where gold has already been found to determine the amount of runoff color—reveals that there is less free gold replenishing the Sandy than the Swift River, Nile Brook, or Gold Brook in Eustis.

Sometimes, when one finds a place that hasn't been worked for years, the results are encouraging. "I've heard of a party going on the Sandy with a four-inch dredge," said Gerald Morrison of Woolwich. "They went to a little side stream that ran through a culvert and got more than a half ounce in a day's time."

The best finds along the Sandy River were near Madrid during the Depression. Since money was scarce and unemployment widespread, people spent more time on the river panning gold in order to buy groceries. Several pockets were found above Madrid by a trapper who sold his gold and pelts in Lewiston. His best find was two ounces taken from a ledge in Sandy River Plantation.

Gold isn't the only precious metal that finds its way into a sluice or pan. Several people have found platinum along the Sandy River and its tributaries. A man who operated a mineral shop below Augusta was convinced that if he dug deeply enough in Peas Stream in Madrid, he would find platinum. This prospector had worked claims in California and had been on the rivers and streams of Maine for a number of years.

Glendon Dill had heard about this mining operation, and one Sunday, Dill went in to see the project. He found a long sluice in the stream but the man was nowhere around.

"I called and called him," said Dill, "but I couldn't raise him. Then I went away from the brook and looked into his tent. He was dead as a doornail."

"He was mining up on the flat, about four hundred yards from Sandy River," confirmed Stanley Voter. "He was building a spot in the river for his sluice when he had a heart attack."

Oberton Stream in East Madrid is not a place that has been prospected much in recent years. Lester Gould and Stanley Voter, both of Phillips, found gold there. "Yes," said Voter, "we used to get a lot of gold out of Oberton by pulling grass roots. But I never found gold in Perham."

There is the story of the forty-niner who saw signs of gold on Perham Stream. He went panning and found several ounces under a waterfall. For a period of two weeks after this strike, the miner was able to average about $14 a day—remarkable wages in the 1850s. After a time, the yield was less. According to some old-timers in East Madrid, this man was always getting gold from Perham and selling it to the local storekeepers.

In 1982, Bill Garrett flashed some vials of Swift River gold to a merchant in Augusta. Instead of being impressed with the three ounces Bill was showing him, the man laughed. "That isn't very much. We get a lot more than that up around Perham Stream!"

When asked who he thought was one of the more successful miners in the Phillips-Madrid area, Stanley Voter didn't hesitate. "Glen Dill found some good gold, but he lost it in a fire. That was something else again. There was nothing left but brown bearings."

Glendon Dill and his wife have prospected many of the rivers of Maine, and they always had a way of finding gold. Nearly every weekend they would go out, either with their pans or with a sluice and pump. For more than forty years, he prowled the rivers. Sandy, Oberton, Nile, Swift, Gold Brook. For a number of seasons he worked his sluice a short distance above Carl Shilling's camp. Glen would drive his jeep across the fording place on the East Branch and down the trail. But the gold he found was lost when the mill he operated in Phillips caught fire and burned. In the fire was a necklace of nuggets that he had a Portland jeweler fashion for Mrs. Dill, a setting with one large nugget on a pendant and five smaller ones on each side.

Tincook, Nile Brook, and Sidney Harden

A hundred years ago, near Greenvale Cove on Rangeley Lake, there lived an old Indian woman known as Tincook. She had no other name; there was no record of where she came from or when she was born. Tincook lived alone in a shack on the left side of the stage road going to Phillips. People called her crazy. When she walked into the village of Rangeley to get the few staple goods she needed, storekeepers quickly waited on her and were glad to see her leave. Some old-timers claimed that Tincook had magic powers and couldn't be trusted.

The stage driver, a Mr. Hinkley, always trotted his horses when he got close to Tincook's shack. It was no place to slow down. The old woman often carried a gun, and she had been known to point it at strangers who foolishly stopped to admire the view on their way to Rangeley.

One day when Hinkley was approaching her place, he saw Tincook standing in the middle of the road. She obviously had something on her mind, and she wasn't about to let him pass. He drew up and waited for her to come to the side of his wagon.

"Mr. Hinkley," she said, "me want you to come into the house. Me show you something."

The stage driver gripped the reins and wondered if it would be best to snap the horses into a gallop. She had never asked anyone into her place before, and there was no telling what the crazy woman would do once she got him inside the shack. Deciding not to bolt, Hinkley nudged his team to the side of the road, got down from the wagon, and followed Tincook up the path.

Once inside, Hinkley stood close to the door and watched the old woman as she reached into a hole in the wall. The stage driver's eyes widened as Tincook brought out a four-ounce jar filled with gold.

"Me got um up Mount," she said, pointing in the direction of Saddleback Mountain.

Hinkley turned the bottle in his hands and told her how nice the nuggets looked. He had never seen so much gold in all his life.

"Plenty mo if me had time to get em," she replied, taking the bottle and putting it back in the wall.

When the stage driver got back into Rangeley that day, he told his friends what had happened and it was then they all remembered that Tincook sometimes would disappear for weeks in the woods.

Not long after this incident, Tincook began muttering to herself constantly, and she shook her fist and threatened the storekeepers whenever she came to the village. Then one day she fired two shots at a man who was passing her place. The selectmen decided it was time to take action. She was examined by a physician and committed to the asylum in Augusta, where she died a short time later.

No one knows who took the jar that Tincook kept in the wall of her shack. Over the years, prospectors have searched the ridges along Saddleback for the place where she claimed to have found the gold. A few flakes have turned up in pans but no sizeable nuggets.

Near the place where Tincook had her shack, on the road to Rangeley, is Nile Brook. In the middle of summer, when the land is dry and wardens are telling campers to watch their fires, there is only a trickle of water under the trees dividing an old cow pasture. But this two and a half mile brook, shaped like the letter Y on the geological survey map, has long been a place of mystery to gold prospectors.

For those who believe that not all the gold in Maine is glacial in origin and a mother lode exists, Nile Brook ranks with the East Branch of the Swift River, Kibby Stream, and the Parmachenee area. Year after year, flakes and nuggets of gold, some pieces tipped with platinum, have washed down in the spring flood. Gold may be thinly and widely scattered in the northern and western parts of the state running parallel with the Canadian border, but here on the east side of Rangeley Lake, only a mile and a half from town on busy Route 4, this precious metal has been heavily placed.

Where is it all coming from? So much gold from a brook with such a short run? Those who spend time searching for its source claim that it is in a clay bank beyond the power lines. Successful miners, like Sidney Harden, Martin Keith, and Glendon Dill, have found nuggets all along this bank. "I could pick gold right off the clay," said Dill. "Pieces the size of match heads or bigger." But go above the clay bank and signs of color immediately fade. "It's got to be there somewhere," said Stanley Voter. "I've often wanted to go a hundred yards in there on the right and dig down with a backhoe and see if the whole area has gold."

The one who did the most prospecting on Nile Brook was "Jake the Trapper." This was long before the turn of the century, around 1880, and several years before the narrow-gauged railroad carried gangs of prospectors to Rangeley so they could dig all summer in the crevices along the brook. It was even before young Luther Nile, owner of the farm, panned enough gold to make his wife a solid gold wedding ring. Every year Jake would travel to Portland to sell his pelts, and nearly always he would bring a poke of gold worth several hundreds of dollars. He would never say where he found his half-gold, half-platinum nuggets, though several people in Rangeley, who knew where his trapline was located and where he could be found most summer days, claimed that Jake never strayed far from Nile Brook.

Years after Jake, another trapper and woodsman prospected there. At the time of his death, this man was receiving assistance, and since he was a town charge his possessions were examined by the selectmen. He had few worldly goods, only clothes and an old trunk. Not finding a key, the town officials broke the chest open. There were the usual things one would expect to find: old letters, some photographs, and mementos from a lonely life. One item did catch attention: it was a bag carefully tucked away, and inside was more than two hundred dollars in nuggets and flakes of gold.

In recent years, prospectors have been keeping up with the gold that comes down every spring. "I went up there a few years ago," said Lester Gould, "and I couldn't believe how they have cleaned it out. I couldn't find any place to work."

Nile Brook has been overworked, but it won't easily be stripped of its gold, unless the source is mined. The clay bank beyond the power lines still yields color and will continue when washed with rain and melting snow. Gone is the time when a miner can find an ounce nugget in the brook, as did Robert Bresbury who carried his lucky find in his pocket, along with his jackknife and spare change. Given a few years' rest, the brook could have another lining of dust; gold washed from a clay bank that yields an endless supply.

Another gold hunter who knew Nile Brook well was Sidney Harden.

When asked to name the best gold prospectors, past or present on the rivers of Maine, those who have studied the scene and mined extensively nominate either Perley Whitney or Carl Shilling. There is seldom disagreement in naming the third person on the list. It is usually Sidney Harden. "Sid had an eighth-grade education and came from Rockland, Maine," said Rangeley historian Edward Ellis. "He got into difficulty as a young man with some teenaged friends, and his father sent him to stay with an uncle who lived between Madrid and Bemis."

The young man loved exploring the woods surrounding his uncle's home, and Harden was often on the old Indian trail in the gore finding arrowheads and studying rock formations along the steep cliffs. Having an inquisitive mind, he learned to identify minerals and taught himself geology. It was inevitable with his wide knowledge of the woods and streams that he would soon begin to earn good wages as a guide for hunters and fishermen.

Harden was born in 1874, and when the mining boom hit Maine he got gold fever, and it stayed with him all his life. Up and down the mountains of Rangeley and Sandy River Plantation and into the Aziscohos Lake region he panned and sluiced, sometimes going north to the Canadian border and exploring the remote streams west and south of Jackman.

It wasn't long before Harden and Martin Keith of Livermore were prospecting together. Martin, who had already found disappointment in the prospect on his father's farm, felt there was a mother lode in Maine. Sid Harden wasn't sure, but he had seen enough to realize that a search for lode gold should be made in the mountains of northern Oxford and Franklin counties.

After a time, Harden gave up guiding and found work as a game warden. It was a job he kept for more than thirty years. Residents of Rangeley remember that he had a forty-five revolver strapped to the steering wheel of his car. It was a regulation required of wardens in those days. Sid still went hunting for gold, and often in the fall he would set a trapline near Swift River Pond in Township E.

Sidney Harden

"He did everything," recalled Edward Ellis. "His facility and interests are clearly recorded among his papers in the Rangeley Library. He received letters from all over the world indicating many different interests."

Archaeology was one of his passions; he collected and wrote papers on local history, and he was recognized by scientists who worked for the State of Maine as an expert in both geology and mineralogy.

"He was very active," said Ed Hamilton of Lisbon Falls, Maine. "I remember Sid came down and prospected our farm for beryllium and found some. He advised my father to hang on to the mineral rights."

How much gold Harden panned and sluiced during his lifetime is not known, but there were sizeable nuggets seen by residents of both Rangeley and Madrid. One vial of gold disappeared. He had the habit of hiding his Nile Brook findings behind a rock near the brook. One day he went back to pan and the gold was gone.

There are people in Rangeley who remember that he would sometimes go into the woods, pull up a bush, carry it back to a stream and carefully wash and knead the roots in his gold pan.

Sidney Harden once told a friend: "There is no prettier sight on earth than a bead of color in black sand."

Gold: West, North, and East of Rangeley

Many of the streams west and southwest of Rangeley have been yielding color to prospectors for years. Leonard Leavitt, known as "The Hermit of Goose Eye," claimed that he found gold at Goose Eye Stream in the wilds northwest of Bethel. It was the summer of 1929, and two Freeport, Maine gold hunters, Everett Smith and Edmund Skillin, backpacked their way into the region to see if Leavitt's report was true. No gold was found on this trip, though the two came home with large quantities of tourmaline crystals. A New Jersey prospector, Myron David, who spent several summers in and around Goose Eye, was able to substantiate Leavitt's claim. A two-week excursion into the area in 1986 produced nearly an ounce of gold for David.

A startling discovery occurred west of Rangeley when the Aziscohos Dam in Magalloway Plantation was being constructed during the Depression. Asad Barrows, who was employed as an engineer on the project, worked harder on his day off than he did during the week. He and several of the workmen went panning for gold in the nearby streams on Sundays. Gold-bearing gravel near the dam site proved to be heavy with color, and some of the panners made as much as $6.00 a day—three times more than their construction wages.

Northeast of Rangeley, in both Dallas and Lang plantations, the streams have been kind to prospectors and to lumberjacks as well. One of the lucky woodcutters was Cyrus Campbell. One day, in 1884, he was out hunting for his lost pick-pole head that he used when moving logs in the river. Campbell wasn't sure, but he believed it had slipped from his pole somewhere near Pondsayer Rapids in Lang Plantation, between Rangeley and Stratton. Following the bank, he came to a ledge where the rushing stream slowed to a standing pool of water. Caught in a crevice was a yellow stone. Prying it loose with his jackknife, Campbell was astonished to find that it was a gold nugget weighing more than an ounce.

For seventy years, efforts have been made by both prospectors and geologists to trace the gold supplying the lakes and streams north of Rangeley in the Eustis area. There are many gold hunters who are convinced that the mother lode is somewhere in the hills of this region.

A vein of quartz measuring ten inches in width and containing substantial amounts of free gold was found by one prospector, and another quartz vein, more than ten feet wide and assaying from $40 to as high as $520 per ton, was discovered nearby.

State Geologist Freeman Burr announced in February 1936 that private exploration had been going on in the Eustis area for nearly a year. The assays indicated that there was enough gold present to assure a better than average return. "Well-known western gold miners operate profitably on ore yielding as little as $18 a ton," said Burr. But Gold Brook in Eustis, promising as it always appears to be, is an illusive body of water. It never lives up to its reputation of being the hot spot on the map.

The presence of gold crystals in pyrite around Eustis is what geologists are interested in these days. It is thought that larger pyrite masses may exist, and if these can be located, the chances are good for recovering substantial amounts of the precious metal. Gold Brook isn't the only place that is getting attention. There is also nearby Alder Stream where two prospectors found nearly an ounce of gold on a weekend trip in 1985.

William Lyons of West Farmington and his three companions dragged a canoe with supplies as far as they could up Gold Brook and went on foot all the way to Sisk Mountain—this excursion was a year or two before Lyons' death in 1982. The men had a sluice with them and came back with more than an ounce of gold. What they found wasn't flake gold associated with glacial activity, but round pitted pieces the size of match heads.

"I had an uncle who went on a wood's job up in the Gold Brook area in Eustis," said Charlie Bragg of Buckfield. "He and two other fellows decided to take a shortcut through the woods on their sled. They were going along and my uncle said: 'God! That looks like gold in that ledge!' And the other fellows said: 'There isn't that much gold in all of Maine!' So my uncle drew off and hit it with the corner of his axe and left a dent in it. That's the honest to God's truth! They went back that spring and the next spring, but they could never find the spot."

Michael Sheridan, who worked for a Washington newspaper, picked up a hiker in the nation's capital. "It was during one of those pleasant conversations," recalled Sheridan, "that the disruptive element of my character—greed—reared its ugly head." Sheridan was intrigued by what he heard. "The man said he and his wife were told by the federal government that a small stream above Eustis, Maine was the best place in New England to pan for gold." When asked what the stream was called, the hiker replied: "A place called Gold Brook."

East of Rangeley, along the southern and western slopes of Mount Abraham, and passing through the village of Salem, Quick Stream tumbles its way into the Carrabassett. Leaving Salem and following the stream to the headwaters, prospectors find themselves in rugged country. The Quick is no slow-moving peaceful run of water. It gets its name for the way it plunges hurriedly to a lower elevation.

Up among the foothills, along the stream, two miles from the village, settlers cleared the forests and built homes. This was in the 1840s when everyone in a family had to spend all day in some useful pursuit to stay alive. Then word drifted back that gold had been found in California. By that time, much of the land around Salem had been cleared, and those destined to succeed had already established themselves in community life. Some of the less successful homesteaders packed their belongings and joined wagon trains or booked passage on ships.

The settlers who stayed in Salem often thought of their friends and relations who had gone to make a fortune in the goldfields, and when they finally got letters telling of nuggets worth thousands of dollars, they began to wonder if there was gold in streams closer to home.

Then one day a settler came into Salem for provisions and displayed a small bag of gold. And where did he get it? He wouldn't say. Those who knew the land around his homestead had their suspicions—they remembered that the Quick ran close to his back pasture.

Several of the villagers hurried to the headwaters and began panning. They weren't expert in swirling their washbasins and frying pans, though they did their best to imitate the methods used by the forty-niners. Before they went home that night, all of them had found color along the banks of Quick Stream.

During the next two months there was excitement in Salem. One settler displayed a nugget estimated to be nearly an ounce, and others found half-ounce pieces. Much of the gold they recovered was in the form of nuggets, probably because they had washed the smaller flakes away when using their kitchen pans.

There was no telling how much gold they found that summer. A modest estimate of its value would be in the hundreds of dollars, which in those days was a lot of money, and an impressive yield for any stream in Maine. Not all the villagers believed the stories circulating in the Salem stores. The more skeptical settlers claimed the gold was planted; they were sure that the nuggets had been found in California—it was just a trick to raise the price of property along the stream.

On the opposite side of Mount Abraham, between Salem and Kingfield, more gold was found. Like the Quick, Rapid Stream empties into the Carrabassett. Few nuggets were panned, but there was heavy black sand with fine gold in the crevices and along the banks. Such traces of color partly silenced the skeptics. After several years, fewer nuggets were taken from Quick Stream, and Salem's first gold strike was over.

For more than half a century, only a few trappers panned the Quick during the summer. It was a way to make money while waiting to work their traplines. Both Quick and Rapid streams now were getting a long-needed rest. The spring thaws had time to build layers of new gold that were washed from the hills and headwaters. Stanley Voter spoke of that time when mentioning how few good ledges had been left on Quick Stream.

"They really worked it then. During the Depression gold was worth $32 an ounce, and the going wage was a buck a day. When a man couldn't find an ounce of gold in a month, something was wrong. They made good money in those days."

A *Kennebec Journal* article, on April 6, 1936, pointed out "the golden side" of the spring floods. State Geologist Freeman Burr estimated that prospectors on gold-bearing streams had moved tons of gravel and sand. For many years, Burr noted, miners had been earning from two to eight dollars a day. Quick Stream was one of the locations. It was having a second Klondike; not only were nuggets again being found but also pieces of quartz laced with spangles of gold.

"I found gold over on Quick Stream," said Glendon Dill, "by the bridge in Salem. I also got what I thought was either platinum or wire silver over there."

Most of the mountain streams in every direction around Rangeley can produce surprises. "A man was fishing on the Carabassett, where the river comes down off Bigelow," said Adam Galuza, "and he found a nugget that weighed an ounce. It was right on top of the ground by a little waterfall. This fisherman swears it. I want to go up there and try that stream."

The Chaudière River, Jackman, and Gold Brook

The Canadians began mining gold on the Chaudière River in the Province of Quebec in 1834, but by 1880 the panning and sluicing had stopped. The accessible places had been heavily worked and the alluvial deposits were presumed to be exhausted. But new locations yielded color, and butchers were still finding small nuggets in the crops of chickens they dressed for Sunday dinners.

Lumberman Paul Bolduc believed that the Chaudière was another California. This sixty-year-old and his wife had mined the river for years, and they had taught their three children how to pan as soon as the youngsters could walk. Mrs. Bolduc kept a pickle jar of nuggets in her kitchen. Since Bolduc had faith in the Chaudière and had gold fever all his life, it wasn't surprising that he eventually got someone to finance his claims. The lumberman found his man in M. J. Boylen of Toronto. In the summer of 1957, they jointly acquired the mineral rights to more than 75,000 acres along the Chaudière. Exploration crews were sent out, and a Quebec newspaper, on February 17, 1958, described the partnership as having "important possibilities." This brought prospectors rushing into the area, some from as far away as Alaska. Many of these newcomers were seen digging through fifteen feet of snow to stake their claims.

Then the officials of Quebec intervened. The Province was worried that an old-fashioned gold rush would develop. Immediately, further staking of claims was prohibited along a forty-mile stretch of the river and a half dozen of its tributaries. The Minister of Mines stated that this action was needed to prevent irresponsible miners from causing floods and jeopardizing the hydroelectric power plants of the Chaudière region.

Further land restrictions were rushed into law as Bolduc and Boylen announced a tentative $2,000,000 operation, to start in the summer of 1958, with money to be raised by public stock subscription. The new Provincial regulations discouraged potential backers, and though some gold was mined in areas recommended by survey crews from Boylen's Toronto office, Bolduc's hope of another Klondike was never realized.

What has gold along the Chaudière River got to do with prospecting in Maine? No one is sure if it will have any connection with future mining in northern Franklin and Somerset counties, but more than $2,000,000 in gold has been taken from claims less than forty miles from Jackman, Maine.

Most geologists and prospectors believe that the gold along the Canadian border in Maine is glacial in origin. No mother lode has been discovered, and since much of the gold on the Chaudière comes in the form of large nuggets and bigger than average flakes, a glacial winnowing may have occurred. All along the border, from the corner of New Hampshire to Grand Falls, where the St. John River enters New Brunswick, sizeable gold has been found.

Perhaps the most spectacular find in Aroostook was at a lumber camp at the head of the Great Machias River, west of Ashland. It was spring and the drive of long lumber was over. A lumberjack, the last in the crew to leave, was walking down a trail to Ashland. He stubbed his toe on a rock, and swearing at his clumsiness, he reached down to throw the obstacle out of the path. A smaller stone caught his eye, and when picking it up he was immediately struck by its weight. It was metal and white. The man had seen natural gold and knew it was heavy. Perhaps this was white gold, he concluded. Arriving in town, he showed the object around, but no one could identify it. Finally, a jeweler examined and weighed his one-ounce find. It was reported to be a nugget of pure platinum.

Theories of a mother lode along the international boundary come and go. As early as 1939, geologist Olaf Nylander of Caribou was saying that there might well be a lode of gold in the northwestern part of the state. Nylander, who discovered valuable deposits of asbestos in Penobscot County, and who gained recognition for pinpointing mineral sources on the Gaspé Peninsula and the Gulf of St. Lawrence, riled several scientists when he used the word "substantial." Most of his fellow geologists believed that there was little of the precious metal in Maine.

Gold has been found in considerable quantities along the headwaters of Spencer Stream, southwest of Jackman, on line between Appleton Township and Township T5 R6. Here men made a day's wage panning gold throughout the Depression.

The best living of all was realized by a trapper from Jackman sometime before 1900. The man worked his trapline during the late fall and winter and mined gold in Dennistown during the summer. No one was able to learn where he panned, but according to several residents of Moose River, he traded the results at the general store and got enough to feed and clothe his family. Frequently, he would appear with as much as two ounces of gold.

Another prospector from the Jackman area made good wages throughout his life. He had a camp in the woods on the road to Parlin Lake, and according to Carl Ellis of Farmington, this man buried gold on the property. "I've always wanted to get up enough courage to go in there with a metal detector," said Ed Hamilton. "Carl pointed out the place to me in 1982."

Canadian mining officials have long claimed that gold extends to the border and into Maine. The problem is that much of the land on this side of the boundary is privately owned, and because there are few roads through the mountainous townships and no chain of ponds, dredgers have been reluctant to face the expense and logistics of getting several tons of equipment into these regions for long periods of time.

Tim Pond, Gold Brook, Arnold Pond, and Coburn Gore were places of much interest to Martin Keith and Sidney Harden. Keith built his own furnace to make assays, and both men believed that important gold discoveries would be made one day in the Eustis-Kibby area.

Sidney Harden was out one day on a fishing and gold prospecting trip near Kibby Mountain when he found an odd rock formation in a dry run. This gully appeared to have been made by the flooding of a nearby stream. As he worked his way down the grade, Harden decided to break open some of the white rock he had seen. Suddenly, a yellow flash caught his eye. A piece of small quartz crysstal had gold about 8xl2mm thick, and when Harden made the fist-sized matrix smaller, it revealed pyrite with traces of gold within the pyrite.

On the geological survey map, T5 R6 and T6 R7 are areas situated in a part of northern Somerset County that is difficult to reach. There is, however, a road to one of the better gold-bearing streams in Maine. Gold Brook, northeast of Gold Brook in Eustis, has long been popular with prospectors.

Most of the miners who dredge this brook claim that they have better luck working the middle of the stream. There is less gold on clay along the banks. When asked if this theory wasn't a generalization, one miner replied: "Go up there and see for yourself." If a dredger strikes what one miner described as brown gravel, color will be hit at once.

"Gold Brook is where I found most of my gold," said Lester Gould. "The last time I went there was six inches of snow on the ground." When asked if it wasn't a bit chilly in the water without a wet suit, Gould smiled and replied: "It was damned cold!"

Gould and Rodney Harnden of Phillips have done their share of mining on Gold Brook. On a lucky day the two found better than an ounce. "We got one of those nice pieces and smaller gold," explained Gould. "After a while, you're bound to hit places where there is a lot. We've probably taken three ounces from that area."

Not everyone has luck. Gold Brook, like any stream in Maine, requires a certain approach if the precious metal is to be found. Glendon Dill remembered a state geologist who made a rocker. "He wanted to show us how it worked and claimed he could get a lot of gold with it," smiled Dill. "We went up to Gold Brook with him. We had to laugh. He tried and tried, but he couldn't find a bit of gold."

Rocks can be terribly frustrating when they get wedged. One prospector found a seam in a ledge going across Gold Brook. In the middle of the stream and at its lowest level, wedged in a crevice, was a rock. "I can wiggle her," said the gold hunter, "but it won't come." Not even a come-along could move it. Since gold was found all along the crevice, one can only wonder what is under that rock.

Often, in heavily worked places, one comes across a small, untouched area. A prospector who does much of his mining on Gold Brook keeps a sharp eye on the more active parts of the stream. "Miners are careless critters," he grinned. "More than thirty percent of the best diggings around are covered by tailings. I always go first where people have been."

How To Pan For Gold

Panning for gold doesn't require expensive equipment. A frying pan or pie tin is sometimes used, though many an amateur panner has worked all day without finding a flake, only to learn too late that gold never stays in a greasy pan. This problem can be easily remedied by burning the grease free over a campfire or baking the pan in an oven. A gold pan is recommended for any person about to go on a prospecting trip.

The standard pan is 16 inches in diameter at the top and 2 1/2 inches deep. The rim is flared, allowing an angle of about 50 degrees from the vertical. Metal pans should be kept free from rust, though some miners insist that a certain amount of rust and pitting helps to capture gold.

In recent years, the plastic pan has become popular, and there are a number of different designs on the market. One criticism that metal pan users have with the plastic models is their lightness. Place them at the water's edge, the claim is made, and before one knows it, the plastic pans are floating away.

Every miner has his or her way of panning. There is no accepted technique when retrieving gold, and what works for one person may not be a satisfactory method for another.

It is important to remember that gold is heavier than most material in a pan. It will settle to the bottom if given half a chance. Let the weight of gold work for you, and never forget that GRAVITY IS YOUR FRIEND.

One wonders why the panning lessons in many gold books are so complicated. It's like trying to assemble a snowblower from instructions written by a person who knows little English. No matter what you do with a gold pan, whether you swirl it, shake it, or bang it against your hand, the gold is going to settle at the bottom. It is your job to get rid of all the lighter material at the top.

A good way for beginners to check on their progress is to add lead pellets of bird shot. If these pellets are still there when one gets down to the black sand, it is doubtful that any gold will be lost.

Here are ten general steps in running a pan.

(1) Fill the pan half full of material and submerge the pan in the stream.

(2) Knead the material in the pan like dough to break up the clay and particles clinging together.

(3) Swirl the pan in a circular motion (clockwise or counter-clockwise) just under the surface. This will discharge some of the lighter material over the rim.

(4) With water covering the material, tilt the pan slightly downward and away from yourself, and shake the pan back and forth to settle the gold at the bottom.

(5) Pick the bigger rocks from the top.

(6) Shake the pan back and forth again, always with some water in the pan to keep the material in a fluid state.

(7) Allow the water in the stream to lap the material in the pan as you tilt the pan downward and nudge it forward.

(8) When you see black sand, shake the pan back and forth to settle the gold and black sand at the bottom again.

(9) Put a small amount of water in the pan, pick up the pan, and streak the water over the black sand.

(10) If there is gold, one will see it as the black sand is slowly being washed aside.

Sluices and Gear

There are dozens of old sluices in the woods along the East Branch of the Swift River. They are built with boards and plywood, and after several weekends in the water, they become saturated and too heavy to carry home. Prospectors park their sluices under trees and bushes, and many leave their crowbars and spades. It's always more pleasant to walk back without a lot of heavy things to carry after a day of gold hunting.

If one does much sluicing, it is more practical to build a metal sluice or purchase one of the many light aluminum models available from prospecting supply houses. An aluminum four-foot sluice weighs about fifteen pounds and can be carried anywhere. A wooden one of the same size, after being in the water for a season, can weigh thirty pounds. Most homemade sluices last only a season or two.

There are a few rules to remember when setting up a sluice. The depth of the water should never be less than four inches, and it helps if there is easy access to the water's edge.

Good gravity separation of gold occurs only when the feed, width and pitch of the sluice and the amount of water are at optimum conditions. The only way to achieve this state is to experiment. The rate of pitch varies, but usually it is between one inch and one and a half inches to the foot. When the sluice is too steep, gold will wash away; when too flat, there will be a buildup of sand. If the sluice is too wide for the volume of water available, sand will accumulate and water will cut channels into the sand; if the sluice is too narrow, the gold won't have a chance to drop to the bottom of the riffles and be stopped. The best action occurs when the material to the sluice is constant.

One can tell if the water is flowing at the proper speed by dropping a small shovelful of material into the sluice. The sand and gravel should break up gradually, taking about half a minute or so when moving with the flow of water. When the material gushes out, the flow is too rapid.

A properly designed sluice should hold about 90% of the gold within the first four to six inches of the box. When one finds gold in the lower riffles, the recovery rate is considerably less. The installation of good carpeting, material with some shag to it, will help to trap the finer particles of gold. No recovery method will capture all the gold; anything over 90% is excellent.

In addition to a spade, crowbar and a pail, one should consider crevicing tools before going out with a sluice. Check the kitchen drawer for old spoons and nutpicks. Medicine droppers make good suction guns for hairline cracks under the water, and tire irons can be used as small crowbars. Almost anything that can reach and dislodge a piece of gold is prospecting equipment. One prospector on the Sandy River had good results one day when using a toilet bowl plunger to loosen material in an underwater crevice.

Hip waders are the best boots to wear if one is moving about and looking for a good place to sluice. If a gold hunter operates in Maine waters for long periods of time and wishes to extend the panning and sluicing season by at least two months, to April and October, the purchase of thick rubber gloves, like those used by electricians on power lines, is recommended.

Different Kinds of Luck

Stella and I realized that we had to change our mining habits if we expected to get more gold. We felt there was only one way to bring us back on the right track. This was to leave our dredge at home.

We walked along the East Bank of the Swift one Saturday and looked at the river as if we were seeing it for the first time. When we did stop to run a few pans for sampling purposes, we tried to visualize what other miners had done before us. After several hours, we stopped to have our lunch by a calm stretch of water. It was not a place that would interest a gold hunter—a fisherman would have better luck here, I thought. The stream ran too slowly to set up a sluice, and then it hit me full force: this spot had never been mined.

A small boulder, resting a few inches in the water near the edge of the bank, caught my eye. Under it was a flat rock, almost like a well cap. I pushed the boulder, and because it was rounded, it rolled easily into the river. The flat rock was next, and by using the crowbar I was able to shimmy it aside.

Just under the water, a patch of clay rose above the overburden. We could see what looked like flakes of color. Reaching down with cupped hands, we scooped a few handfuls into our pans. The place was crowded with fine grains of gold.

We stayed all afternoon brushing aside the gravel that covered the clay, and when our hands became sore we found an old can and used it as a bailing tool. We got nearly a quarter of an ounce from an area of a square yard. It was time to bring in more equipment. We finally had found a suitable place for our dredge.

Instead of getting into our wet suits the next morning, we kneeled in our waders and worked the suction hose in the shallow water along the edge of the bank. There was a strip of clay about four feet wide and twenty feet long. It yielded more color than the square yard patch we had bailed the day before. We spent all afternoon removing the thin layer of overburden and dredging the small flakes of gold stuck to the clay. To rest our backs, we cleaned the riffles of the dredge and panned the concentrates whenever we had to fill the tank with gas. By nightfall, we had an impressive vial of gold. We dragged the dredge into the woods, covered the tools and engine with a canvas and walked back up the trail.

We spent the rest of the summer dredging along this bank and digging gold from the crevices. Our only fear was that we soon would attract a gang of gold hunters, but that section of the East Branch looked so uninteresting to others that we were left to ourselves. What we liked best about this fifty feet along the river was the consistency of color. There was gold in every pan, and whenever we walked back from a day of mining, we felt well rewarded for our efforts.

It was after our fifth gold season that we decided to sell our home in Mount Vernon, Maine. We were ready for a change in our lives. I restored our old farmhouse that winter, and by spring we had a customer. We placed most of our personal belongings in storage, and by early May we had moved into the little two-roomed camp which we rented from Clarence Bateman and which had been built by Carl Shilling. It was good to be back on the mountain in Byron.

We were there only a week before I had one of my most memorable prospecting experiences. There was a ledge on the East Branch which had always fascinated us, and every year we would go there two or three times and spend a few hours panning. Since we didn't want to dredge several days running, the ledge made a pleasant change.

I was digging a reddish clay from a crevice when I saw what appeared to be a small vein of springwater coming from an open space in the bank. I got my long-handled spade and filled the pan with this reddish material. I hurriedly swirled the pan at the edge of the river and carelessly brushed aside the larger stones. I was so convinced that there would be nothing in this sampling that I didn't wait to get down to the concentrates. I stood up to ease a sore back muscle and fanned some water across the gravelly clay. What I saw took my breath away. There in the pan was a nugget the size of a quarter in diameter and round as the end of my thumb. I stood looking at it for nearly a minute before speaking.

"Stella," I said in a quiet and even voice, as if nothing in particular had happened, "maybe you better come and look at this."

She knew me well enough to know that I had luckily come across something worth seeing.

"We're rich!" she shouted, jumping up and down. "We're rich!"

Those moments still rise in my mind, and as I carefully placed the pan on the ledge so we could safely study the nugget together, I knew there would be few gold mining moments that would equal this one. The nugget, sizeable for any Maine gold, was more than twelve pennyweights.

Surprisingly, I didn't have to wait long for another memorable experience. It came within a week. We were down on the East Branch working the crevices near the place where we had found gold on the clay. An insignificant crack in a ledge opened to a hidden crevice that was about six inches long, an inch wide, and two inches deep. I carefully scratched and spooned the material until the bottom of the crevice was cleaned. There were two handfuls of black sand and reddish clay when I began to run the pan. As I streaked water over the concentrates, I saw a Milky Way of color. It wasn't just a peppering but a half teaspoon of gold. I gathered this find in pinches for the vial and thought it to be more than a quarter of an ounce.

Nuggets found by C. J. and Stella Stevens

We weren't the only ones to find gold that summer. I saw two cars parked above Bateman's camps, and curious to see what was going on, I parked my truck and walked in. Bill Garrett had three beginners with him, and I could tell at a glance that something unusual had happened.

Bill was sitting on a rock in the stream, and he was panning faster than his usual speed.

"What's up, Bill?" I asked.

"That fellow over there should be in Las Vegas," he replied with a noticeable edge to his voice.

I looked over by the ledge and saw a middle-aged man clumsily shaking a gold pan back and forth at the water's edge. I waited until Bill was ready to tell me the story.

Bill had taken the three to the ledge and had shown them how to pan, and when they seemed to understand the principles, he started panning for himself. Two of the men decided to dig in the clay near the water and the third began breaking open crevices high on the ledge. They worked for nearly an hour, the two by the water getting a few flakes, and the beginner higher up finding nothing.

Garrett went over to the man who was panning the upper crevices, and what Bill saw nearly jolted him out of his waders. Clinging to the rim of the pan, about to plunge into the water, was a pennyweight nugget.

"Don't move!" said Bill as he grabbed the pan. "That's gold!"

"Oh?" said the beginner. "Is that what it looks like? I thought it looked like something else." And before Bill could reply, the man went on. "I had something like that a couple of pans ago, but I thought it was just a rock."

Bill and the other two went through all the tailings, but there was no sign of the nugget.

I stood talking with Bill for several minutes, and just as I was about to leave, the man on the ledge came over with his gold pan.

"I think it's another one," he said in a normal voice. "A bit bigger, don't you think?"

Bill Garrett stared at the gold pan for a long moment before answering.

"I'll give you a hundred dollars for it."

The man looked at Bill and down at the nugget. I could see he was more interested in gold mining now.

"I guess not," he replied. "I'm going to hang on to this one."

A Conversation with Charlie Damery

Charles Damery was a man with many friends. Employees who had him as their foreman at Polaroid Corp., neighbors up and down the streets in Old Orchard Beach, Maine, and miners who met him on the river all cared for him. He had a way of showing people not only how important it was to be alive, but how good it felt. His curiosity and openness was a pleasure to witness. He looked upon strangers without suspicion, and inevitably saw only the good side of a person. Stella and I were always amused at Charlie's way of identifying parties who drove up the mountain to pan for gold. They would be "the folks from Massachusetts" or "the folks tenting down Bateman's Lane." After visiting Charlie, while walking back to our camp, we would sometimes improvise. "Oh, those are the folks on death row" or "Aren't they the folks who burned the little village?"

Charlie always called Stella "Young Lady." He was terrible with names, and it was all too obvious when he made introductions.

He loved to talk about glaciers, and when I mentioned tertiary channels he was delighted. He was convinced that the source of gold for much of the East Branch of the Swift River came from the hill across the road. "I can close my eyes and imagine the glaciers," he grinned. "Just think of a great sheet of ice taking the top off Tumbledown!"

It was sad to see how much he wanted to spend all day working his sluice in the mudflat near his place. Charlie's heart was in a terrible state at the time in his life when we met him. He was well aware of it, but he wasn't going to allow self-pity to overshadow the pleasure of living. Once, when several of us were finding sizeable nuggets on the East Branch two miles from his camp, he walked all the way down and back on a hot August day to see what was going on.

Charlie began visiting Byron in the mid-fifties, and it wasn't long before he and Clarence Bateman were close friends. Bateman sold Charlie some land, and together they established a tree farm.

"He was one man who was nice to Carl Shilling," said Helen Barker. "One summer my sister and I needed some work. We were living in Bateman's camp. Charlie hired us to cut the brush going to Carl's camp. Often, during the day, Charlie would be singing Christian songs to us. Why, it would lift you right up!"

He had been active in the Salvation Army for years, and it would be difficult to find a person better qualified than Charlie as a soldier in such an army. It gave him extreme personal satisfaction when he could be helpful to others. Sometimes he would have a "star boarder" at his camp; some miner who had no place to stay on the mountain. These lonely gold hunters always knew that Charlie would put them up for a night or two and give them plenty to eat. "He's not a bad person," Charlie would say when it was obvious that his guest was taking advantage of him.

In a lighthearted mood, Charlie Damery was the irrepressible child. He could throw his entire body into a delightful pantomime to describe an amusing situation. I remember one visit he made at our camp. It was the morning after a bear had broken the porch screen to grab a bag of garbage I had left overnight. Charlie got down on all fours in the grass and began sniffing. Up the wall of the porch he sniffed, grunting with bear-like satisfaction, and finally he reached one hand through the hole in the screen to struggle with an imaginary Glad Bag.

He was very conscious of his lack of formal education. He would frequently tell of his difficult childhood, how once he got into trouble as a young man, and that he found the Christian way and spirit that gave his life shape and meaning. All this would be said before he launched into a long conversation about mineralogy or natural science. He loved carpentry and planning improvements in his camp. Then he would share some amusing little story, such as the night he and Bateman sat up until dawn before they got a photograph of two raccoons in a bird feeder in front of Bateman's camp.

Charlie loved coming to Byron and spending a few nights whenever he could get away from Old Orchard Beach. As his heart grew weaker and trips to the hospital by ambulance more frequent his wife, Rose, became alarmed. They were now selling their home and moving to a retirement apartment. Perhaps it was also time to sell the camp; he and Rose had talked it over and it seemed the sensible thing to do for people in their mid-seventies. Charlie could still come to the mountain for visits and could stay next door in the place he had given his grandson, Chuck.

I shall never forget Charlie's first halfhearted attempt to place the property on the market. It wasn't just giving up a camp he had built: for Charlie, it was relinquishing all those years of dreams and discoveries. But there was still an edge to the man and his humor. "For Sail" read the barely legible six-inch by three-inch board staked only six inches above the ground beside the road in a bed of weeds.

"This is for you, Young Lady," said Charlie Damery on one of our last visits. He was giving Stella his mortar spade, one that was light to handle and could dig in narrow places. "You need a thing like this up here on the river."

DAMERY: Welcome to my humble cottage. May the sun that shines by day lighteth your path by night and everlasting happiness and the path you travel with gold.

Q: Thank you. While we're on the subject of your cottage, I'll begin by asking: How did you happen to come up here?

DAMERY: I got talking with a fellow by the name of Max Field Parrish. He worked with me at Polaroid, and he had a great interest in gold. "If you want to do some mining on your vacation," he said, "then go to the Swift River in Byron." I thought that was a wonderful idea, and he lent me his gold pan.

Q: Did you know how to use it?

DAMERY: I had no idea how to pan. But the first person I met was Dean McCrillis. He took me out and taught me how. McCrillis had a little mineral shop by the cemetery in Byron at that time—Dean was one of the better miners around. Then for several years I rented either the small or big camp from Clarence Bateman. Eventually, I bought some land from Bates (Bateman) and built my own place. I've been coming here now for more than twenty-five years.

Q: Do you think the gold in Maine is glacial, or do you believe there is a mother lode?

DAMERY: I'm not going to accept anything now, after seeing the nugget you found the other day. How much does it weigh?

Q: A little over half an ounce. About twelve pennyweights.

DAMERY: I can't believe it is one piece of gold. It's got to be two individual nuggets tied by some mechanical force. I will not buy it any other way—not in this river and the action I've seen. How can there be so much big gold down the East Branch below Carl Shilling's camp and so much small gold up river?

Q: But there is small gold down below Carl's.

DAMERY: Yes, I know. But how does it get bigger? I have seen this river when the ice is breaking up. It took the bridge out one year on the East Branch.

Q: Charlie, you are not answering my question. What about a mother lode?

DAMERY: The indications are that there has to be a supply of gold to fill these beds on the East Branch year after year.

Q: What about the West Branch of the Swift River?

DAMERY: I read a letter that Mrs. Ferrin (Thelma Ferrin) got from two German gentlemen. They wanted to come to Byron and set up a mill to crush and grind the rocks on the West Branch. They thought it would be profitable. Why they never came, I don't know.

Q: We know there is an old placer mine where Carl Shilling built his camp, but why so much gold above this placer site?

DAMERY: It's a mystery. But I've always had a feeling that much of the gold by Carl's might have come from the mountain across the road from my camp, and it washed over the mudflats. There's an awful lot of iron up there—we know iron is associated with pyrite and this is gold bearing in minute quantities. A lot of small gold is found on that mountain, year after year.

Q: Isn't it true: When you get to the clay you will find gold?

DAMERY: You would like to believe that, wouldn't you?

Q: All I'm saying is I do find gold at bedrock and on the clay. But when I go under the clay, I sometimes find gold that hasn't moved much and has sharp edges. Probably gold from another glacier.

DAMERY: Yes, I've seen that. A glacier spread out the clay and all the material on it. But big floods brought in the rocks afterwards.

Q: There are people who believe that the gold in Byron comes from Tumbledown Mountain, and others swear that the mountain was once a volcano. But a geologist assured me that there is an absence of volcanic rock.

DAMERY: I have in my collection what I believe to be a volcanic button. I found it in the East Branch. I went to a mineral meeting once, and they showed pictures of these buttons. "My heavens," I said, "I've got one of these at home. It's incredible!"

Q: There are those who claim that the pond at the top of Tumbledown was once a crater. You don't believe that, do you?

DAMERY: They never found a bottom in that pond. But any theories you may have will be blown out the window when you look at your gold under a microscope. You'll begin to see that some of your pieces of gold are very strange looking little critters. The fact that I only went to the third grade in grammar school puts me at a terrible disadvantage. You asked me where I thought the gold came from—I'm still trying to put it into perspective.

Q: So are the so-called experts, Charlie, professional miners and geologists. If they knew where the gold was located, they would be there this moment.

DAMERY: I tell you what you want to do. I'll bring the microscope up and you make some slides. Get a can of hair spray to set your slides and clean your gold; then study your mounts up one side and down the other.

Q: And I will begin to say: Oh, here is some gold that hasn't traveled far. Now where did it come from?

DAMERY: You're talking like an interesting miner now. You want to know some answers about things we both don't know.

Q: But we quickly get into trouble when we prospect with preconceived ideas. If we're not flexible and imaginative on the river, we waste a lot of time.

DAMERY: It's mind-boggling, this river. One year I came up here and brought bottles with me and took samples all the way down the East Branch at different locations. I put them on slides and numbered them. But I wasn't able to come up with anything. Yes, you're right: once you think you know a thing, you begin to know less.

Q: I read somewhere that if one plants horsetail, there is a chance of getting gold.

DAMERY: In a gold area. There are small sacks on the roots that absorb these small fine particles. The pod on a horsetail is minute. They are of the fern family.

Q: Any horsetail in Byron?

DAMERY: Just up the road. I've dug some up and washed the roots and found traces of gold. But why does horsetail all grow on one side of that road and in patches? I don't know what causes that.

Q: It's interesting how quickly a river can shift and open new channels after a storm or in the spring flood.

DAMERY: All the time, moving back and forth. The greatest movement I ever saw on the East Branch was below the bridge at the end of Bateman Lane. Overnight, the river turned forty-five degrees. There have been so very many serious floods up here—even cars trapped in the river.

Q: A lot of gold has been taken from the East Branch over the years, but not in huge amounts at one time.

DAMERY: A young man from Montreal, a French fellow—I can never remember names—he was supposed to have found some gold two summers ago.

Q: His name was Claude.

DAMERY: Claude! He said he got two ounces of it working just below Carl's camp. His word is as good as gold—what else can you say? I do know he worked long hours dredging. I used to see him going down early every morning with his gas can. If you handle the sand and gravel, you can get the gold. But not always in one place. There can be some unusual changes in the rock that will leave a place naked as a newborn babe. Yet ten feet above that spot, it can be filled with fine particles of gold. How big an area did you work? That place halfway between Carl's and the Main Branch?

Q: An area three square yards.

DAMERY: How deep was it?

Q: We went to bedrock. In places it was only four inches, and in one spot four feet.

DAMERY: Did you get much gold?

Q: In one five-hour day we broke ledge, scraped the clay and dredged the entire area and got a quarter of an ounce. That was our best yield down there.

DAMERY: Clay is very funny stuff: it has a texture to it and it doesn't always break. The old-timers used to put it down through a hollow log. Then they would hit the log and roll it about—this broke up the clay. After that, they ran it through the master sluice. In other words, they were imitating the action of the river.

Q: I've always been astonished how soon a dredge hole in the river can fill again. Spots I dredged last year would appear untouched to those who are just beginning to prospect.

DAMERY: You have to learn what to look for in a river. If you find a beer can or leaves, forget it. Whether it is hard packed or not, it might have been moved by certain changes in the water pattern. You have to learn about gravel. There is a never ending battle when checking for signs.

Q: Rocks often lie in the line of least resistance if they haven't been touched.

DAMERY: That is underwater. Above water, I can show you a perfect illustration. Stand at the bridge that crosses the East Branch and look around. All the big rocks are on one side, and all the sand in another spot. That place has been dug out year after year, but every spring you go back and it's filled with the same kind of sand. A perfect example of sorting, sorting, sorting.

Q: Dredgers don't always go to bedrock—they get discouraged and they stop. You see too many holes on this river where they went down only a foot or two.

DAMERY: Like a squirrel starting to dig a hole. It thinks it can go no further and starts over in another place.

Q: What makes you think there is gold coming off that mountain across the road from your camp? Isn't this wishful thinking on your part, Charlie?

DAMERY: We all believe that gold is formed in quartz. There is a formation up there that is unique. You need to go to the bench mark and head straight south, and you'll see the greatest formation of quartz you ever saw in your life.

Q: You feel that a lot of gold washes down off that mountain?

DAMERY: I know it does. For years, we've panned the bank at the end of Chuck's lane. (Charles Smith, his grandson) We'd always get two or three flakes. For the last four years, I haven't gotten any there. In fact, the river has changed and moved further down, but it keeps distributing gold behind certain rocks. My brother and his boy were up here panning, and I said: "Dig behind those rocks there, for the fun of it." He came up with three nice pieces of gold.

It didn't surprise me.

Q: Reading the river in the spring is important.

DAMERY: Unless you are up here in the spring to see the way the water runs, it would be very hard to do many experiments or to guess where the gold comes from or how it gets here.

Q: Have you found any platinum?

DAMERY: There is platinum here. I found a piece. Bill (Garrett) weighed it and gave me a name of something else—I forgot what he called it. But I can't accept that. Specific gravity isn't always perfect, and I raise the question to the density of this material.

Q: Do you think that much of the gold is pulverized after it leaves Coos Canyon on the Main Branch?

DAMERY: I would think that is what happens. If gold drops into those holes down there, it will be pulverized. Those potholes are more like a mortar than anything else. As Carl Shilling always told me: "You've got to break rock and dig in the muck! It's in the muck!"

Glaciers and the Mother Lode

Maine has a layer of sands, soil, gravels, and clays which varies from inches to about a hundred feet in thickness. Below that is found the bedrock of the earth. This rock is unpredictable and highly variable. Our technology for mapping the material is still primitive—we know so little about how it was formed. Maine's mining boom collapsed when richer veins proved easier to get at in the western part of the country. Successful mining activities have been carried out in Maritime Canada, only a short distance from the border, but not in Maine.

It was during the Pleistocene Period, from 15,000 to 300,000 years ago, that one of our most important events in geological history occurred. This was the ice age. Boulders on Mount Katahdin indicate that the ice sheet covering the state was at least 7,000 feet thick. These glacial advances were followed by warm interglacial periods similar to the temperature we experience today.

The grinding power of the ice has left its mark. U-shaped valleys and rounded hills surround us. Many of our mountains have glacial scratches where rocks embedded at the bottom of the glaciers were dragged across bedrock. Some geologists believe there were as many as four to six different glaciers in the Pleistocene Period and others say two. We do know that one of the glaciers topped the mountains, and another advancing sheet of ice reached about 2,000 feet along the sides of elevations.

The tremendous weight of the ice sheet pushed Maine downward about 400 feet. After one ice age, the sea came inland as far as Skowhegan, Livermore Falls, and Fryburg. When the ice retreated, the land started rising, the uplift being greater where the ice was heavier. A pressure of approximately 155 tons per square foot, caused by one mile of ice, defaced New England. It is not known if the release of this pressure after the ice age is accountable for earthquake tremors, but this part of the country wasn't free of them. New England had a cycle of tremors between 1620 and 1840. The area was shaken 231 times, and Boston was heavily damaged by one of these earthquakes.

The two glaciers that caused the distribution of gold were the ones that took off the tops of the mountains and ran southeast and due south. Then why shouldn't there be lodes of gold still left below bedrock? Aren't we placing too much emphasis on glacial activity? Dense gold has been found only forty miles north of Kibby Stream, on the Chaudière River in Quebec, and one of the biggest gold strikes in the Western Hemisphere occurred not far from Maine, at the Bancroft Mines in Ontario. Geologist Forrest Dexter, who doesn't think Maine has a mother lode, was quick to respond to this question.

"That strike up around Bancroft was in ancient rock. That gold was 1.8 billion years old." Reminded that gold doesn't conform to boundaries between countries, Dexter replied: "But it does conform to pluton boundaries." (Plutons being bodies of intrusive igneous rock.) "When these granite bodies were in place, they cooled very thoroughly, and they were invaded again and again with hydrothermal quartz."

When it was hinted that he had better be careful or his interviewer would be hopelessly lost in a scientific quagmire, Forrest Dexter smiled and went on: "If you feel there are more minerals to be obtained, you go around on the north side of the pluton. It's around the fringes of the pluton that you get the high mineralization." Asked to give an example of a pluton, he replied: "Take the White Mountains. That is a gigantic pluton. It is totally bared by the glaciation, and the quartz is on top. That granite was once ten thousand feet below the surface."

Dexter didn't appear surprised to hear that there had been recent reports of gold found in Norridgewock. "It all depends where it was found. The sea came in at Norridgewock. If you go out on the airport road, about a mile from Route 2, you get to some sand pits where you will find blue clay. That's marine clay." Then Dexter pointed out that the hydrology maps—maps showing the water sources—were revealing. "You will see that the aquifers (water-bearing stratum) run from the northeast to the southwest. It hits the coast roughly at right angles. You've got those, and they had a lot of glacial melt with channels. They came down with high velocity in sands and gravels."

Martin Keith always believed that there were economic possibilities of gold in Maine. There were too many earth formations in the state identical with those in Canada for him to think otherwise. "You want the ancient sediments that have been first laid down by water and then tilted up for this kind of hunting," said Keith. "At Swift River above Rumford, for example, you'll see the rocks edgewise, schists and metamorphic structures, and that's a sign of lurking gold."

"I'm going to split my answer," said Greg Willet, when asked if he thought there was a mother lode or if all the gold was glacial and from Canada. "I have found it in mineralized veins, and we also deal with a large amount of glacial gold in this area."

Greg Willet got interested in mining while growing up in Maryland. He was convinced that the forty-niners didn't get all the gold. Willet taught himself how to pan, and after operating several claims in the West, he moved to Maine. His prospecting excursions have covered much of the northwestern part of the state, as far down as Farmington, north to Gold Brook, and in the Parmachenee area.

"I have seen gold in quartz," admitted Forrest Dexter, "but I've never seen it myself in any Maine quartz. I've had people hand me pieces of Maine quartz, but I'm not at all sure of their veracity. If there is gold in it, I suspect they got it from somewhere else."

State geologists and mining experts as a rule are not optimistic about a rich concentration of placer gold in Maine, and most of them believe there is no mother lode. They think gold prospectors are fooling themselves. Between the U.S. Geological Survey and the Bureau of Mines, explorations and reconnaissances have blanketed Maine and the Swift River area in particular. But these surveys are often conducted by people who know little about using a gold pan and how to locate gold.

One survey was conducted by Elbert Pratt and Henry Condon along the Swift River watershed, between Roxbury and the Height of Land, covering an area of about 100 square miles. This reconnaissance was made in the summer of 1946, and the purpose was to gather data on gold placers. The exploration was carried out by panning the streams and using a sluice box at intervals along the river. From reading their notes, one can see that they shoveled underwater material into their pans (a sure way to lose gold) and that they had no system in the selection of their sites. If they found nothing after a few pans, they concluded that there was no gold in that location.

"There is little gold in the Swift River below the East Branch which can be recovered by simple panning methods. The West Branch and Berdeen Stream show relatively few flakes of gold as does the upper Swift River above Houghton."

This report would come as a surprise to the hundreds of miners who have found nuggets and vials of gold in these locations since 1946. Pratt and Condon ended their report with no real enthusiasm for gold hunting.

"There is not enough gold in the streams of Swift River Valley, even the East Branch, to support mining as a business. Men from the gold country of the West tried it without success. But for those who want a sample of gold and some exercise, it is not too difficult to clean out a few breaks in the ledges to get the gold dust. Some may be lucky enough to find a larger specimen."

To paraphrase one Maine geologist: Only men who are dreamers will spend all day swatting Maine blackflies while looking for a mother lode of gold. Prospectors aren't always scientific when developing theories, but they have had more experience in sensing where gold can be found. There are still many dreamers who believe that somewhere between Byron and Coburn Gore or Bethel and Jackman, in some place untouched by man, there is a pocket of gold heavier than a weightlifter can shoulder, and with nuggets big as a giant's fist.

Swift River Gold

One of the reasons why the Swift River has been the favorite location for gold miners is that it easily can be reached. Motorists can get out along Route 17, and the Main Branch is only a few steps away. Logging roads and trails run for miles along the other branches of the Swift, and the more adventurous panners can follow footpaths made by fishermen.

The East Branch has always been the most productive stream in the area with the Main Branch a distant second. Some sizeable nuggets have been taken from the West Branch, and there are a few prospectors who prefer to dig there. Kenneth Knapp and his son, Lee, have long favored this stream. Although the Stockbridge Branch has been a disappointment to miners in recent years, Berdeen Stream and Mott Brook have yielded nuggets of more than a pennyweight, and many of the hillside brooks are washed with color every spring.

Miners from all over the country come to Byron, and on any weekend during the summer one will see several cars parked along Route 17 and beyond Dingle Hill on the back road to Weld. Joe White, who lived across the road from Coos Canyon, saw miners come and go. He rented gold pans, crevicing spoons and small sluices for years. White also gave instructions to novices who stopped to see the rock collection he had outside his house.

It seems incredible that there is any gold left in the Swift River. For more than a hundred and thirty years the banks have been lined with panners, and when the river gets shallow in dry seasons, dredgers prowl the middle for untouched bedrock. "Though nothing has been found to justify more than recreational panning," said geologist Walter Anderson, "it wouldn't surprise me at all to see somebody run across gold up there. It's the right kind of setting; the right kind of geology for somebody to find a primary precious metal deposit."

One person to make a careful study of Swift River gold was Benjamin Burbank of Brunswick. Not only was he a chemist, metallurgist, prospector, and geologist, but he became one of the most respected mineralogists in Maine. "He was a rare Leonardo da Vinci," said a Bowdoin College professor. Rarely did a week go by that Burbank's opinion wasn't solicited by someone in the field of mining. When he retired from the Bath Iron Works in 1964, Burbank catalogued the entire mineral collection at Bowdoin College. "A previous curator, in his great wisdom," as one professor at the school explained, "had taken all the rocks and had thrown them into boxes."

One of Burbank's uncles, a forty-niner, got Benjamin interested in gold panning around the state. This uncle did a considerable amount of prospecting on Quick Stream in Salem, and on one trip he found a nugget weighing more than a half ounce.

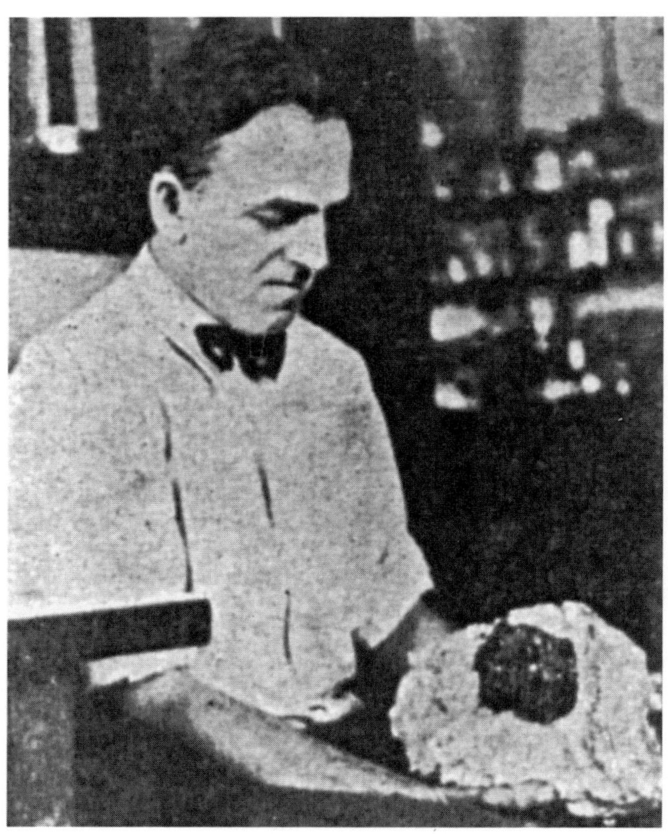

Benjamin Burbank

Burbank, who served as President of the Maine Mineral Association for a number of years, became interested in gold and minerals before graduating from Bowdoin in 1926. Park Cleaveland tutored the young Burbank, and together they went on tourmaline hunts in southern and western Maine. Burbank's first love was prospecting for gold. He found nuggets on the Swift, and there were few streams in Oxford, Franklin, and Somerset counties that he didn't explore. Some of the gold he found on the Swift can be seen in a wall display in the geology department at Bowdoin. Specimens from the East and West Branch are mounted on two squares of black velvet.

In some places on the West Branch, less than a half mile from the gate on Route 17, pieces of gold the size of match heads have been panned. One Rumford resident dug a quarter ounce of gold from a ledge in three hours. The strangest find of all from the West Branch appeared in Kenneth Knapp's gold pan.

Dean and Ann McCrillis with Sons George and Phillip, 1961

"It was the size of a pea," said Knapp, "and it was very very heavy. I gave it to Dean McCrillis for him to test in Roxbury." McCrillis was unable to identify it, and Knapp nearly forgot about it. "One day I saw Dean and asked him. 'I hope you didn't want that for anything, Ken,' he said. I told him I didn't, but I was curious about it. He explained that it was in the Smithsonian Institute. *They* didn't even know what it was. It's foreign and grayish in color—a dark, dark gray—and very heavy. An element alien to earth."

It was a common practice in the 1920s for Swift River prospectors to sell their finds to Rumford jewelers. Jewelry made from pure Maine gold was in great demand. It was also a time when the precious metal was popular for both teeth and fillings. The badge of the Sheriff of Oxford County is made from Swift River gold, and three necklaces owned by the state museum also contain gold from Byron. One of these necklaces was donated by the Maine Jewelers Association to the state museum with the understanding that it could be worn by the wife of the governor on important occasions. Mrs. James Longley made use of this necklace several times, and whenever the newspapers carried stories of her wearing the jewelry there were more gold hunters along the banks of the Swift.

Newspapers have long looked to the Swift River for unusual copy. The tale about gold found in the crop of a chicken has been used in scores of gold mining articles around the state. Sometimes, in slanting the material, reporters stray from the facts. In 43 gold articles, mention has been made of a mother and her two daughters who earned a living panning and sluicing on the Swift. This material originated in 1941 when Harry Packard wrote a long piece for the *Portland Telegram,* published on October 5, with the headline: "Panning Gold in Maine Stream Aids Woman to Educate Daughter." The article, along with photographs of Thelma Ferrin and her two daughters, Helen and Irene, wasn't really about Mrs. Ferrin getting enough gold to send her daughter, Irene, to Mexico High School, or to buy the pretty clothes that Packard claimed the girl needed. The piece was mostly about panning and sluicing and what backbreaking work it can be for those who spend all day on the river.

Helen Ferrin Barker

Helen Barker, one of the daughters, was unacquainted with the story, nor did she think of herself as a participant. "No," said Mrs. Barker, "I never did know about those people."

A more interesting article might have told how Thelma Ferrin and her husband, Frank, got gold fever one summer and spent most of their time prospecting the East Branch. Lee Knapp, Helen Barker's son, recalled this gold hunt.

"Grandfather had one summer when he did nothing but prospect," said Knapp. "He and Grammy went in on the East Branch, and they tried to trace the gold." Knapp said his grandfather claimed that gold was like a funnel: the further from the source, the more color; the closer, the less. "They went up there for six weeks, day after day after day. The only time they came out was to get food. My grandfather told me that when he stopped—because of cold weather—the gold was getting scarcer and he was getting nearer."

Rudolph Bartsch of Brookline, Massachusetts took his annual gold mining vacations in the late summer and early fall of the year. He made more than a dozen trips to the Swift during the 1950s and 60s. Bartsch chose that time because the river was lower and bedrock could be reached easily. He believed that many pockets of gold were left after the glaciers sheared the tops of mountains. "I dig where the water runs from the hills," he often told people on the river. Bartsch, who was President of the Boston Mineral Club and a man who knew his geology, found some sizeable gold. He never could equal the ounce piece found by Carl Shilling, but Bartsch did get a nugget weighing more than a quarter ounce. "I never came up with a pan that didn't at least show color," Bartsch once boasted. "I believe there is more gold in Maine than there is in California. That's why I keep coming here."

The best gold location for Adam Galuza was the Stockbridge Branch. He set up a sixteen-foot sluice and scraped the first two inches of gravel from a clay bank. "I filled two small aspirin bottles with flakes as big as oatmeal," said Galuza, and chuckling, admitted that what is left of his lucky find now rests in an unusual place. "My kids were playing with those two aspirin bottles of gold when I came home one day. 'Look, Dad, don't that shine!' " Galuza caught them several times with the two bottles until there was only a bottle of gold left. "So I opened the cap, threw the gold on the bedroom floor, and swept it down the crack. That's where it is now. Still under the bedroom!"

Too many tales about people finding nuggets on the Swift River have circulated, and because Byron gets much of the attention, many productive streams in the state have gone unnoticed. When a Bethel, Maine man told how an elderly relative rigged up a sluice and supported an entire family all one summer, the banks of the river had more traffic for weeks. There are also stories about couples covering expenses. Some do, though many come to the Swift and return home with only a small vial lightly sprinkled with flakes.

"Most of the gold seekers in Byron are just out to have fun rather than to make money," said Lee Knapp. "They claim that the Byron gold is the purest around. It's fun to get out and look for it, and it's a good clean hobby." Knapp, who has helped panners for a number of years, believes that more gold is being found today than in the past. "All they had years ago was a pan, a shovel, and a pick." Then Knapp concluded: "Every once in a while, somebody will find gold where it shouldn't be, and it shoots their theory to hell."

Swift River: Where East Joins Main Branch

An Interview with Harvey Packard

I always had the feeling that I was about to find the mother lode when I went prospecting with Harvey Packard. Whenever my energy level got low, or I was thinking of other things while on the river, Harvey's enthusiasm for prospecting renewed my interest in what might be found in the next gold pan.

We were usually in pajamas and having breakfast by our tent at the campsite known as the Lean-to as he drove by. He never stopped to talk in the morning; he was in too much of a hurry to set up his sluice and to look for the big gold.

Q: Do you really think there is a mother lode of gold in Maine?

PACKARD: I believe there is a geological fault running down from the Rangeley area. A huge crack somewhere in the earth. Down below Carl's there is a spot on the East Branch where you can look both upstream and downstream and see bedrock, but in one particular area you don't see any. I dug a hole there and went through three feet of clay. Under the clay, I found jagged pieces of quartz—I think this is tertiary gravel. The geological survey will tell you there isn't any, but there is in that particular area. Wherever it bottoms out, I believe there is a large deposit of gold.

Q: We both have found nuggets weighing more than a pennyweight in this location, and what interested me was that they were found on a line. Dig nearer the bank, you would find nothing; dig closer to the water, you would have no luck.

PACKARD: And when I first found those jagged pieces of quartz on that line, you know what else I found there? Round balls of grayish clay. I found it right in the gravel. I think this means that somewhere upstream, during a high water or flood, some of that clay blew out and washed on a line down that stream and got packed in that tertiary gravel. Then some rocks slid down and covered it all.

Q: How did it blow out?

PACKARD: Here. Look at these. (He brings out two pea-sized buttonlike stones) These are pure jasper, and in my collection I had one white one. A fellow who was with me on the river dropped it into the stream and it got lost. But there is no way that these stones going around in that area could be made into that shape. Those jaspers were pushed up through a cold hydrothermal vein—that's why they are that shape. These things were pushed into a spiral and up. And where I found the jasper, I found this (shows a button of iron magnetite) and I found these.

Q: Those are sizeable nuggets of gold!

PACKARD: Yes. And under a microscope they all have quartz.

Q: Are you still digging there?

PACKARD: Oh yes! Don (Don McBurnie of Hampden, Maine) was there last summer in exactly the same spot where he was the summer before, and he was getting nice big nuggets on top of the clay. They are on the top because they are washing out. Somehow, they are being blown through.

Q: How far down do you think you would have to go to find this large deposit of gold?

PACKARD: I have been trying to find out. The only way is if someone took a machine up there and they drilled. One would really have to take a core sample and pan it to find out what is down there.

Q: There are more than seventy-five old gold mines reported in Maine. But there seems to be a band of gold that is richer and running parallel to the Canadian border. Most geologists claim that it is all glacial gold.

PACKARD: I believe in certain places there are deposits of gold. I have the proof: bismuth, platinum, and gold. I talked with a man who lives at the head of Rangeley Lakes. He said two geologists from Washington, D.C. told him that there was a 1,500 foot sheer off, which would point to two geological faults. In California the larger amounts of gold are found on the fault areas.

Q: Have you ever found gold on the Main Branch of the Swift River below Coos Canyon? Or is it pretty well ground up?

PACKARD: Flattened. I once found a piece the size of my little fingernail below Coos Canyon. It was in a book standing up in the river. I pulled it back and just peeled it off.

Q: Do you usually have to move a lot of overburden before you find gold?

PACKARD: I once made a hole above where Garrett used to take his people, above the power lines on the Main Branch. The land belongs to Dean McCrillis, and he gave me permission to work there. Another fellow and I went with a small dredge. I followed the ledge on the bend, and I kept going down, moving all those rocks. I went down about eight feet and came into hard blue clay. We ran for two hours before something happened to the motor on the dredge and the place filled up with water so all the work I had put into that hole was over. But we managed to get three pennyweights of gold, and it was getting thicker and thicker.

Q: What do you think of metal detectors?

PACKARD: Some metal detectors won't pick up your gold. I've got one, and I know if I put all the gold on this table on the floor and went over it, it wouldn't read.

Q: Do you think you can find gold by dowsing?

PACKARD: I was told by two or three people who go up to the river that there is some magnetic force that draws me, like if there was a gold nugget around, I would be drawn to that area.

Q: A sort of psychic power?

PACKARD: Now this is on my own. With the literature I got from Harvard and piecing together what I knew, I telephoned Kay Morris. She's a psychic on the radio, and you can call her. I didn't mention anything about gold, but I just said I had lost something. She hesitated a little and finally said: "You go upstream and you'll see a log in the water and right there is where it will be." I went up, and that is where I found all of this stuff. But another thing: this particular area is where I believe the geological fault comes out. Right there.

Q: A river snakes back and forth. When you dig in the dry beds, do you find much gold?

PACKARD: It doesn't work. It's no good. Why? Because you're not going deep enough, and you are in what I would call an ancient stream channel.

Q: Why don't you sometimes find gold in the classical places? Did someone get ahead of you?

PACKARD: I would say probably.

Q: What signs do you look for when you prospect for gold?

PACKARD: Well, you take this nugget right here; it's just about a pennyweight. I read in a miner's journal—this was after I found some in a straight line below Carl's—go downstream on the bed and measure ten feet. So I measured exactly ten feet and cleaned a crack in the ledge and the nugget was there.

Q: Regarding gold dredges, do you think dredging practical or just some toy for people to play with on weekends?

PACKARD: As far as getting gold, I would say dredges are impractical. If a person is doing it for enjoyment and has the money, I think it's fine.

Q: How do you feel when you see a nugget in your pan or sluice?

PACKARD: It makes you feel good. It's been around a long time, and you are the first person in the world to have seen it. That's quite a thrill.

Dowsing for Metals and Minerals

Four hundred dollars is a lot of money to pay for a dowser when a person can easily make one out of two coat hangers, but the stainless steel chamber and extension antenna on the Anderson dowser appealed to us.

I'm a water dowser, though my abilities aren't developed enough to determine how far down one must dig before striking a vein. I have had strong readings, enough to double a stick and to break it in my hands. What I can do is locate water generally and with some accuracy.

We bought our dowser for the purpose of hunting gold and minerals. I don't think we really expected to find the mother lode with such an instrument, but we enjoyed using it while out mining. Stella has more faith in the practice than I have, but I get stronger readings. If a person thinks wealth will come immediately by using a dowser, he or she is in for a disappointment. This isn't a shortcut to a vein of gold.

I got very poor response from professional dowsers around Maine when researching this book. They knew nothing about dowsing for metals and minerals. Two of them enclosed literature on dowsers they wanted to sell me, and I heard no more from any of them.

I met a gold prospector who had some luck with dowsing. It was

Greg Willet in Rangeley. "I do believe in dowsing from the respect of one's own mind," Willet told me. "If you believe in what you are doing, there is an energy within one. If the mind says *yes,* then it does work. I will say my dowsing was responsible for one of my claims out West."

We found that the dowser was helpful as long as we did not expect more than being led to a general area. Our readings usually matched. With our eyes closed and unaware of the direction we were facing, we did get the same results, even when we used the different lengths of our dowsing rod.

It's easy to get sidetracked, particularly when you allow your feelings or hunches to get in the way. Without an open mind and confidence in what you are doing, dowsing is a waste of time. I'm not positive enough to be a talented dowser: my negativism often gives me false readings.

Stella and I went dowsing with Harvey Packard one day in the Hartford, Maine area. Harvey, who has talent as a dowser, was trying to locate tourmaline in a ledge in the woods. It was a place he remembered from his childhood. The mosquitoes were thicker than I had ever seen them, and we were being badly bitten. I was getting a different reading from Stella and Harvey, and since mine was more definite, they decided to follow my dowsing direction. What I located wasn't a pocket of tourmaline as they stumbled behind me over a fence and into a berry patch. It was a beeline through the woods to our vehicle. My desire to get away from the mosquitoes was stronger than my urge to find tourmaline.

An Incident Downriver

We lived with the sound of rushing water in the background on the mountain in Byron, and sometimes at night the East Branch seemed to take on a life of its own, as if it were breathing. Then when it rained, the river threatened—it had the roaring sound of a beast, and we were aware that it could be deadly.

Stella was visiting her father in London, and because I was by myself and planning to work a ledge downriver early the next morning, I left my dredge in the water. I had tied the machine to a tree with a piece of clothesline. When I woke at dawn and heard the rain, I cursed myself for being so careless. I knew it was only a matter of time before the rope would snap and more than a thousand dollars' worth of equipment would break up on the rocks.

C. J. Stevens

I drove down Bateman's Lane to the landing, got into waders, and studied the river. The water was rising but not rushing fast enough to take me off my feet. I decided to cross by the landing, run the two miles down the old railroad bed, cross the river again, and pull the dredge up on the bank. This seemed quicker than going through the woods.

I made excellent time down the trail and was relieved to find the dredge still tied to the tree. But one glance was enough to tell me that the water was higher now, and as I listened I realized that the roar was noticeably louder. I came to the decision that it would be better to cross a hundred feet above the dredge where the water was usually shallow.

I started across, and even as I edged my way on a downriver slant to avoid meeting the current head-on, I knew I was risking my life. The water broke over my waders before I reached halfway. Then it dawned on me that I was alone and no one was there to pull me from the water if I lost my balance and hit my head.

When the river reached my belt, I knew there was no turning back. The rush of water was forcing me more and more on a slanted course. Twenty feet below me was deeper water and further down several irregularly-shaped boulders.

Holding my breath, and leaning into the full force of the flood, I kept inching forward like a tightrope walker. Twice, I nearly fell. Then, just when I didn't think I would make it, a rise in the ledge at the bottom of the river brought me into shallower water. Gasping for breath, I rushed to the other side.

After pulling the equipment out and covering the engine with a canvas, I took the long way home through the woods with the roaring sound at my back.

Some People on the Swift

We spent two summers in the little camp on the mountain in Byron, and we got to know dozens of miners. Prospectors come from all professions, but when they get together the main topic of conversation is gold. We enjoyed sitting on the tiny screened porch in the evening and watching the fireflies and chatting with river friends. "Just where do you think that the mother lode is located?" someone would ask, and all would join in and talk about the chances of finding it.

We liked most of the gold hunters on the mountain, though I do recall two or three who got on my nerves. One of them was friendly enough, and he wanted to be liked, but he had one deplorable habit: he sponged on everyone. I remember driving to the end of Bateman's Lane one morning, and while I was getting my mining gear together, he came out of his camper in his underwear. It took him only a moment to see my thermos. "You've got coffee!" he announced. "I'll have some of that!" I barely nodded as he went to get his cup. The receptacle he returned with looked bigger than a water pitcher. "I've been wanting some of this since I woke up," he told me. Then he emptied my thermos, and without a word of thanks he shook the last drops into his monstrous piece of crockery. "Nothing like coffee to get a man started in the morning," he said gruffly, going back to his camper.

There was one gold hunter who never had any luck. It was painful to watch him, week after week, coming back to his camp with only a trace of color. "Here, try alongside me," I told him on several occasions. This didn't change things. I kept getting gold in my pan, and he came up with nothing. At first I thought he must be doing something wrong, perhaps some careless motion when panning the concentrates. But no, the man had a better technique than most on the river. Then one day, finally, he found a crevice packed with flakes of gold. He carefully stored them in a glass vial and proudly brought them back to camp.

The next week two of his friends attempted to play a trick on him. They climbed on the roof of his camp and closed the chimney with a cap, accidentally knocking loose the stovepipe. The vial of flakes fell from a shelf and was broken. No one on the mountain was surprised to hear that most of his gold disappeared through a crack in the floor.

After talking about a woman who walked into the river with a gold pan while dressed in silk stockings and high heels, Adam Galuza tells a hard luck story. "I was picking gold from my pan," said Galuza, "when a couple passed by, came to a screeching halt, backed up, and wanted to know what I was doing. So I told them.

'God!' they said, we've been panning all day and haven't found one piece!' 'That's funny,' I said. 'What have you got for a gold pan?' 'We've got a screen,' they replied. They thought they were going to get nuggets in a screen with a one-inch mesh!"

Even without the need to stake a claim on most of the rivers in Maine, gold hunters get into the habit of returning to the same locations. Territorialism plays a part in mining. Stanley Voter recalled how those who usually went panning or dredging down Bateman's Lane felt out of place when mining at the other end of the river.

Stella Stevens dredging

A prospector who had never ventured further than his roadside mining operation decided one day to walk the trail below Carl Shilling's campsite to see if the stories he heard about nuggets of more than a pennyweight were true. This miner had no luck panning, and he felt uncomfortable all the time he was downriver. It just wasn't his territory. On his way back, he counted every step he took, partly to convince himself what a waste of time it all had been, and to assure himself that he would never walk that way again.

Not all miners on the gold scene get along together. "There are two from New Hampshire," recalled Richard Minear, "who go to the Main Branch of the Swift. The one who gets there first gets the upside ledge, and the last one gets the downside ledge. They will sit with their backs to one another and throw rocks at each other."

Every miner develops a personal style and way of retrieving gold and of getting equipment downriver. Among the more innovative hunters on the Swift are Ed Allen and Robert Bird.

Ed Allen has been coming to the East Branch for many summers, and he finds his share of gold. Ed, who lives in New Hampshire, and who has mined on Baker Stream and the Wild Ammonoosuc in his home state, prefers the Swift. Of all the prospectors on the mountain, I found him to be the most ingenious. The contrivances he has invented to get his equipment up and down the river show imagination. In recent years, like so many miners, Ed has had less need to be creative and playful. He now uses an ATV with a trailer.

Robert Bird, who came to the East Branch frequently in the early 1980s, and who had mined in Alaska, had the most unusual sluice of anyone around. He just wedged a piece of carpeting between rocks in the river and began shoveling. The flow of water over the carpet did the rest. Whenever Stella and I saw him, we'd smile and say: "Oh, there's Mr. Bird with his magic carpet!"

Bird always did things differently. If he saw a crack or a seam in a ledge or boulder, he wouldn't get out his pry bar and try to widen the opening. Instead, he would fill a bucket and begin flushing. In no time, flakes of gold would appear at the lower levels where they could be reached.

Then there was "Paul the Puller." We never did know his last name, but we had heard other miners call him Paul. The "Puller" part came about because he had the habit of sitting in his van with the window partly open and with his arm pulling steadily at his rearview mirror. At other times, the grip was on an imaginary beard.

Paul the Puller was the first one to arrive on the Swift during the three years that he came to Byron. He would come in March when there was still ice in the river. He had a cot and camp stove in the van, and his living room was behind the steering wheel where he would sit for hours watching the Main Branch and the passing traffic along Route 17. After the snow melted and the mud roads were dry enough for travel, he would go up over Dingle Hill and park along the East Branch. The Puller was anxious to have the mining season begin.

But he would have to wait for the water to warm up a little. Then when the blackflies came in late May, he would postpone his mining until after the dragonflies were out in full force. Unfortunately, these insect helpers never made their appearance all at once. There he would sit patiently behind the wheel, hoping that the season would begin soon.

Stella and I stopped one day to say hello, more out of curiosity than friendliness. He told us that he had been "putting the hurt on flies"—pulling off their wings and keeping them prisoners in a matchbox for a time before releasing them. We hurried on our way, glad to have the visit over.

Paul the Puller stayed until October. He was hoping that there would be a few days of Indian summer when there were no insects around. He never had much luck; there was now a chill in the air, even in the sunshine. When the leaves began rusting around him along the East Branch, the Puller felt it was time to leave. Where he went, we never knew, and he never came back after that third year.

Then there was the miner who visited us once and stayed half the night. "For your edification," he would begin, "you will find there is more gold on the east side of the river or brook." The man had been lecturing for nearly three hours at our campfire. "Now when I was working behind that big boulder up on the Main Branch"—I closed my eyes for a moment, knowing only too well what he would say next—"I'm telling you this for your own edification."

Finally, when he stuck his nose into a fourth cup of coffee, I asked him: "If you know so much about looking for gold, why do you find so little of it?" My question didn't phase him. He took several gulps and went on as if I hadn't spoken.

It was past midnight, the campfire had only a few coals and faces were difficult to see, before the man got up and went down the lane with his flashlight.

Stella and I often play a game with names; names we give people. I am reminded of the woodsman who explained to us that the tree he was cutting had a rotten heart. "I wonder whatever became of Rotten Heart?" one of us would ask. And there was the mechanically-minded man who called a piece of machinery "the most beautiful thing you ever saw"—his was a long name. I was almost asleep when I heard Stella say in the dark: "We just met Edification."

I don't know if one would call it gold fever or plain foolishness, but there were two men who appeared in Byron convinced that they were going to make their fortunes. The two had left their wives with relatives in Iowa, and had driven all the way across country. They had heard that a person could make as much as $3,000 in a weekend by panning gold on the Swift River.

The trip got off to a bad start before the second day. They decided to come to Maine by way of Canada, and at the border the authorities found a pistol in the trunk of their jalopy. The gun was confiscated, and they were fined $500. This took most of their grubstake, and they barely had enough money left for gasoline. By the time they reached Byron, both were starving. They only had one gold pan, a spade with a cracked handle, no waders, and not even a container for all the gold they expected to find on the river.

Charlie Damery fed them, and Bill Garrett lent them another pan and spade. Then Bill gave each a gold vial. The two worked all weekend and found nothing. Finally, Garrett took pity on them and taught them how to use a gold pan properly. It wasn't until the middle of the week before they got the necessary funds from their wives to make the long journey back to Iowa. When they left Byron, they had five flakes of gold between them.

Coos Canyon: Jerry and Rosey Perrier

For more than a hundred years Coos Canyon has been a jumping-off place for those who seek gold. Located on Route 17, the highway between Rumford and Oquossoc, in the town of Byron, Maine, this small picnic area overlooking the spectacle of a waterfall is where gold hunters congregate before wandering off for a day on the Swift River. On the right, facing the falls, a narrow bridge spans the canyon. Many dreamers and cabin fever sufferers have crossed here in springtime to follow the road over Dingle Hill and on to the East Branch of the Swift. There is no denying it, this is where the bigger nuggets hide on beds of clay and in crevices. Up Route 17, heading north, one soon crosses the West Branch. There are panners who think that outcroppings of gold will one day be found along the hillside further up where the water is only a trickle between boulders. If not there, maybe on Berdeen or Bemis Streams. Somewhere, the more stubborn panners and dredgers insist, a mother lode is wrapped in a shroud of quartz.

In recent years, Coos Canyon has been a convenient stopover for those eager to learn the fundamentals of recreational mining. Jerry and Rosey Perrier began giving panning lessons in 1990 when they started a campground just beyond the falls. They had no idea that the art of swirling a gold pan would become an important part of their newly-opened mineral shop and campground business. It happened to them much in the same way it did to William Garrett fifteen years earlier. Bill began by sharing his mining techniques because those wanting to learn were so enthusiastic. Without realizing it, he was soon caught in the gold traffic; strangers were at his door, all in desperate need of mining supplies and instructions. Finally a decision had to be made: either say no for the sake of privacy or go commercial.

Rosey Perrier was four years old when she first held a gold pan. It wasn't unusual to get such an early start—all ten of Joe and Mary White's children were taught to find gold. With parents who had one of the larger displays of minerals in New England, prospecting became for her a way of life. The family had moved from Massachusetts to Byron in 1948. Wherever Joe White traveled, he picked up stones—even during World War II. "I remember my mom talking about the time Dad came back from Africa and brought rubies with him. We all collected," said Rosey. "Dad and my brothers would go on weekend trips and come back with a truckload of minerals."

Rosey Perrier

Prospecting wasn't part of Jerry Perrier's childhood. When he left the Upper Peninsula of Michigan and bought the house next door to the Whites, Jerry had never heard of gold mining in Maine. The idea astonished him, but he soon got the fever. He remembers vividly the atmosphere of comradery shared during an outing with the White family and friends—thirty or more excited gold hunters along the bank of the Swift River.

Jerry Perrier

Over the years, Joe White taught hundreds how to pan, and he was respected for his ability to locate color. He could read the river. This was a skill he shared with Carl Swantee, Perley Whitney, and Carl Shilling—three well-known Byron prospectors. (Rosey Perrier recalls Shilling. "I was really young, but I remember him coming to the house one spring with that white beard and long white hair." Her father gave Shilling a haircut and Rosey sat on Carl's lap. "I was scared to death. I thought he was Santa Claus.")

Joe White enjoyed dramatizing his panning adventures with the Boy Scouts. "My dad would take them to the old gold mine," Rosey recalled, "and have one of my brothers sneak ahead to the cave." (That small chamber on a cliff by the river was the site where the shotgun charge of gold flakes was fired into a quartz dike in one of Maine's more colorful mining swindles.) When the Scouts arrived for their day of panning, the ominous growl of a bear could be heard coming from the cave—they all scattered screaming. "Dad did that for many years. Then a kid ran into a little tree and knocked himself out. Later that summer another Scout shouted: `Don't worry, I'll take care of that bear with my jackknife!' and rushed into the cave. I guess it was then Dad decided not to do that anymore."

Mining fascinates the Perriers. Simply expressed, Rosey believes "gold is where it's at." There are the traditional places, such as inside bends and where the water slows. But husband and wife are believers in hunches. If a particular place seems to beckon, one should try there first. Asked if they thought there was a mother lode of gold in Maine, both had doubts. "If I found one," said Rosey, "I would leave it there and forget about it. There is the mystery of trying to find out where gold is coming from, and this is something I wouldn't want to lose."

A pennyweight is her best gold find, and Jerry recalls the day that he led several of the campers to a lucky spot where they took "400 salt-and-pepper-sized flakes" from a small hole in a ledge. Translated into dollars, the wage would be pitifully meager, but they all shared in a wealth of excitement. "It is so relaxing when you are panning," explained Rosey. "You think about the gold that may be in the bottom of your pan, and you forget everything else. The fun part is the anticipation."

Jerry is convinced that women find more gold than men. "I see it all the time," he explained. "It's always the wife and the kids that are outdoing the guys when we take families panning." Rosey does find more than her husband, and he is proud of her intuition on the river. So many times he has gone mining with no results until she arrives. "Have you tried here?" she will ask. "And sure enough," says Jerry, "there will be gold in the next pan."

Two large bins have been placed outside the Perriers' mineral shop, and it is here their customers receive instructions. "We get five dollars per person," said Rosey, "concentrates are provided, and the one receiving the lesson gets to keep the gold. We also rent gold pans and teach sluicing." Her pennyweight piece of gold wasn't one that she could keep—she and Jerry have never strayed from their sharing rules. "That nugget was at the end of a sluice," remembered Rosey. "I kept looking at it and thought: Gosh, would I like to have that for my shop! Finally I picked it up and gave it to the guy."

There are twenty campsites at the Coos Canyon Campground, and the Perriers have no plans for expansion. They want to protect the natural beauty of the surroundings along the canyon. Each campsite has a picnic table, a fire pit, a bench swing, and a marshmallow toasting bench. The sites are marked with signs for all the animals in the area. "Lost Beaver Boulevard" is in memory of a poor beaver that lost its life on the icy river in a spring runoff. What gives vitality to the campground is the thrill of the gold search. "Did you see the nugget so-and-so found?" "I sure did! It was nearly half a pennyweight."—This is the sort of exchange Jerry and Rosey hear when they visit their campers on a Saturday night.

When gold is mentioned, both Perriers become animated. They are well acquainted with the river and are sensitive to its changing moods. With their mineral shop, campground business, and part-time jobs, this is a busy couple. He plows snow for the Town of Byron, maintains cemeteries and bridges; she is Town Clerk and a professional carpenter. It is a crowded lifestyle but one that many a gold hunter would envy—"a dream come true," says Rosey.

Ona Willet

Ona Willet, who is registered with the Rangeley Chamber of Commerce as a gold instructor, has prospected Maine waters for more than a decade. For eight years she has taught beginners how to achieve the rhythmic swirl of a pan and where to find hidden crevices and layers of clay—years that have made her more sensitive to the secrets of the river. Ona learns as she teaches. "There are many intuitive things that get said," explained Willet. "People sometimes are so excited they fall backwards into the river; then I'll hear someone say: 'I never saw you like this before!' " These first-timers never leave disappointed. Everything is provided on these outings: vials, pans, digging tools; better still is the promise of finding gold—her personal guarantee—and flakes "of such size that you don't go away with eyestrain."

Prospecting isn't limited to panning excursions; there are dreams of other adventures now that she has become a licensed scuba diver. When asked why that, Willet replied: "I can't stand being at the surface of the water looking in." Formations at the bottom of rivers and underwater overburdens interest her. Would the diving activities be restricted to gold mining? "I may treasure hunt in other directions," she answered. "There are a couple of sunken boats in Lake Champlain that I find intriguing."

Ona Willet was born in Massachusetts, but a number of the early years were spent in Thailand and Pakistan and there were frequent trips to Europe. Her father, a civil engineer, and her mother, a registered nurse, took Ona and an elder sister with them on even the smallest of journeys—"we had a lot of worldly exposure."

Ona left home when she was fifteen, "a renegade" who hadn't completed high school. Because she was too young to be legally employed in the workplace, Willet created her own job. "I was a housekeeper," she explained, "but I didn't clean just anybody's home. I went for the professors, the artists, the lawyers—people I wanted to be around. I absorbed their lifestyles." She also got to audit classes at Colby, Thomas Business College, and the University of Maine-Orono as partial payment for her cleaning services. While trying to get an education Ona became fascinated in photography, especially laboratory work, and for a time she operated a photo lab to supplement her income. But it wasn't all a life disciplined for self-improvement; she needed to be part of the excitement of her times.

Ona Willet with her daughter Tasher

"I came off-the-cuff of the sixties," said Willet when recalling those years, "and throughout the seventies I was sort of subcultural, in-so-much as the music had been the most common binding thread in my life. I was with rock bands and folk rock bands and with musicians."

When asked whether she was a "spirited" gold hunter, her response was immediate and emphatic. "Committed!" her voice lifted.

A young Tasher Willet panning for gold

Then she recalled a dream she and her former husband, Greg, had of one day persuading highway construction companies to screen all their gravel through a sluicing system before using the material on roads. The gold waiting in deep pits and bedrock crevices should not be lost in the paving of streets.

Willet hedged her reply when asked whether she thought that Maine had a mother lode. It was possible that some boulders sliding down from Canada during the glaciers were laced heavily with the precious metal. "Somewhere there is gold spitting out, very fresh and new." She has found color more than once in crevices that had been cleared the year before. "But if there were any substantial amounts, somebody would have located it, and we would have heard—there are no secrets to be kept for long here in Maine."

One of her favorite streams is the West Branch of the Swift River. She has prospected its length but prefers to hunt gold further back on the hillside. "I try to get away from the others," she explained. People often ask Ona if she finds being by herself in remote areas intimidating. "Never," she tells them. "If I should find myself too far out to get back to my vehicle before nightfall, it wouldn't bother me."

"Every time on the river is exciting," said Ona Willet. "The quest is intriguing, and there are no parameters." She is convinced that there is more to gold hunting than the search. "It is when you need to go sit by a river somewhere to make it all work—this is when you find the magic."

Reading the River

A flake of mica at the bottom of a brook on a sunny day can easily fool a person. "Is it or isn't it?" the beginner will ask when staring at the unidentified chip. The two important questions are: Will it break? Does it bend? The best test is to scuff the flake across the pan while applying pressure, and if still in doubt, see if an indentation can be made with a knife or pin.

Gold can be found in more than ninety percent of the surfaces of the earth. One can take a sample just about anywhere, and with spectrographic analysis or X-ray detraction find traces of the element. Since Christopher Columbus and the beginning of opening trade in the Western Hemisphere, gold has been found in nearly every country in the world and in almost every state—some three billion ounces. But it isn't mined always as a primary metal. More than one-third of all the gold produced in this country is a byproduct from mining other deposits, such as copper, lead, and zinc. Perhaps less than ten percent of the gold in the United States has been recovered. Nobody knows where the next mining rush will take place.

Gold never glistens under reflected light nor does it change color. It won't rust, and it can be coated with an alloy of another metal, such as iron, copper, manganese, and oxides of other metals. Gold sometimes has a lighter tint due to the presence of silver. Its atomic weight is 197.0 and its specific gravity is 19.3. In addition to being a major medium on international monetary exchanges, this precious metal has been prized for jewelry and other adornments. Its purity in the jewelry trade is scaled as 24 karat (24k) is 100%, 12k is 50%, and the very popular 14 karat is 58 1/2% pure.

Early man probably was picking up gold nuggets along streams even before the discovery and use of copper. The golden fleece of Jason is no legend. Prospectors, several thousand years ago in what is now Turkey, found that the fleece of a sheep made a good gold trap when placed underwater in a stream. And *gold* is mentioned more than 400 times in the Bible.

The shine of mica in a brook isn't the only thing that will mislead the beginner. Another, and more sophisticated trickster is pyrite, better known as "fool's gold." Like mica, pyrite can be tested by scraping it in the pan while applying pressure or scratching its surface with a sharp instrument.

The first thing a person should learn when panning for gold is *how it performs.* Since it is among the heaviest materials found on Maine rivers, gold quickly settles to the bottom of the pan. Another "heavy" is magnetite, commonly called black sand. This is sulfide iron material and magnetic. Beginners should remember that placer gold is found in and associated with magnetite.

Gold is often discovered at the edges of whirlpools and at the tails of eddies, on the downstream side where there are tributaries entering, in streaks or layers along sandbars, on inside bends where a draw meets the bedrock, and on the downstream side where there are obstructions. Color is sometimes plentiful below the intersection of an ancient riverbed. The rougher the gold appears, the nearer the source; the smoother or rounder gold is, the more it has traveled. Gold will accumulate at the head or foot of a bar, at the bottom of a rapid where the water is slowed, and on bends where the current is reduced. A certain amount of gold will be washed down a river and be deposited in crevices and pockets that were mined the previous year. It is a good idea to recheck the places that yielded the most gold after every spring flood.

Ordinarily, gold doesn't travel far from its source. If one finds irregular pieces, it is wise to proceed up the stream taking additional samples. This doesn't indicate that there is a lode nearby; scattered irregular pieces of glacial gold are common on Maine rivers.

Gold and coarse gravel can be moved only when a stream is running rapidly. On curves, where the water slows its motion, gold collects in sand and gravel. Since gold is about seven times heavier than the material which accumulates on these beds, it quickly settles in pockets and irregular low points. Beds with angular-shaped gravel—these easily can be identified by digging test holes—rarely contain gold; gravels that are rounded, and have an abundance of black sand, garnets and quartz pebbles, should be examined closely. As gold moves downstream, it is gradually released from the accompanying rock and flattened by the persistent pounding of gravel. In time, flakes and tiny particles are formed as the flattened pieces break up.

Maine winters are helpful in freeing gold. As ice forms it pushes the rocks further apart, and this allows more water to get into crevices. This constant freezing and expanding acts like small explosions in slow motion.

Many prospectors on the river have definite opinions of where and how gold can be found. Don't expect precise locations and rules to be repeated for long because gold hunters constantly change their minds. Perhaps it is more accurate to say that they keep up with their disappointments.

One must never allow tradition to dominate mining habits. Don't be afraid to look in places that other gold hunters ignore. Being flexible is often the quickest way to pay dirt, and one of the first mistakes made is to allow room for generalizations. Playfulness is a prospector's greatest strength when trying to unlock the mysteries on the next bend in the river.

ABOUT THE AUTHOR

C. J. Stevens is a native of Maine. His poems, stories, articles, Dutch and Flemish translations, and interviews have appeared in approximately five hundred publications worldwide and more than sixty anthologies and textbooks. He has taught at writers' conferences and seminars and has lectured widely. He is the author of *Beginnings, Circling at the Chain's Length, Hang-Ups,* and *Selected Poems* (poetry); *Lawrence at Tregerthen (D. H. Lawrence in Cornwall)* and *The Cornish Nightmare (D. H. Lawrence)* (biography); *The Next Bend in the River (Gold Mining in Maine), Maine Mining Adventures* and *The Buried Treasure of Maine* (history and adventure); *One Day with a Goat Herd* (animal behavior); and *The Folks from Greeley's Mill* (fiction). Stevens has lived in Malta, Ireland, England, Holland, and Portugal.